DAYDREAMS THE FARM ON MUDDYPUDDLE LANE

Heart-warming, uplifting romance

Etti Summers

CHAPTER ONE

The bus pulled into the pretty village of Picklewick and drew to a halt. Maisie Fairfax clicked up the handle of her suitcase, tied the belt of her jacket more firmly around her waist, and got to her feet. Bumping her suitcase down the steps of the bus, she rolled it to the side of the pavement and reviewed her options.

She had two: walk the three kilometres from the village to the farm on Muddypuddle Lane, or phone her sister and beg a lift. Neither held much appeal. Getting a lift would be preferable to pulling her suitcase all that way, but she wasn't sure she could face Dulcie's ire. Which was why Maisie hadn't informed Dulcie that she was coming. If Dulcie had known beforehand, she probably wouldn't have let Maisie come.

In some ways, Maisie wouldn't have blamed her. Maisie knew she could be unreliable, but that was only because she hadn't yet discovered what she wanted to do with her life. Dulcie didn't understand her, that was all. Unfortunately, neither did their mother, which was why Maisie was turning up at Dulcie's farm unannounced on this chilly afternoon at the beginning of March.

Dulcie wouldn't be amused, but neither would she send her packing. At least, Maisie **hoped** she wouldn't.

No, Dulcie couldn't – there wasn't another bus back to Thornbury today (Maisie had checked) and even if Dulcie drove her to the train station herself, Maisie doubted whether they would get there in time for her to catch the train back to Birmingham.

She gazed around the high street. Many of the shops had already closed for the day, although a small convenience store was still open, and a fish and chip shop had several customers waiting in line. The thought of battered fish and hot, fluffy chips made her mouth water, but despite having only had a latte and a chocolate chip cookie since she'd left Birmingham this morning, Maisie knew she had to save her money until she managed to find another job.

Lights were on in The Wild Side she noticed, but she guessed that Otto, Dulcie's other half, would be too busy getting the restaurant ready for its first customers of the evening to spare the time to ferry her up to the farm. Besides, Maisie knew that asking Otto to give her a lift would irritate Dulcie even more, and her sister would be irritated enough already.

There was always the option of phoning Nikki, who lived just off the main street, but Maisie's eldest sister would be even more annoyed than Dulcie. Maisie did consider asking Nikki if she could stay with her, but Nikki's cottage only had two bedrooms and both were occupied, so unless Maisie wanted to sleep on the floor, she had no choice other than to go to the farm.

Sod it, she would just have to call Dulcie and get the lecture over with. She would have to face her sister's wrath at some point, so she may as well do it whilst being chauffeured to the farm, rather than when she got there. At least she would have saved herself the walk and spared her arms from being yanked out of their sockets if she had to drag her case up the steep hill.

With a resigned sigh, Maisie took her phone out of the back pocket of her jeans.

Her sister answered after a couple of rings.

'Hi, Dulcie, it's me.'

'Maisie! Hi!' Dulcie sounded surprised. 'Is everything okay?'

'Er, not really.'

'What's wrong? Is it Mum?'

'Mum is fine.' And Mum would probably continue to be fine until she realised her youngest child had done a runner rather than face her disappointment when she learnt that Maisie had lost yet another job.

'Thank goodness for that,' Dulcie was saying. 'You had me worried for a minute.' There was a pause. 'If it's not Mum, what is it?'

'I need a favour,' Maisie said. 'I'm in Picklewick – can I have a lift?'

There was a stunned silence, then, 'Why are you in **Picklewick**?'

'I'll tell you when I see you. Can you come fetch me?'

Maisie could almost sense Dulcie's eyes narrowing as her sister asked, 'Does Mum know you're here?'

'Not exactly.'

'Oh, Maisie! Have you been sacked again?'

Maisie heard Dulcie's exasperation and resented it. It was alright for her: Dulcie had landed on her feet when she'd won the farm on Muddypuddle Lane. She'd had it handed to her on a plate. Plus Dulcie had never had to do a job she loathed for minimum wage. **And** she had lucked out when she'd met Otto. He loved her to the moon and back and treated her like a princess. None of Maisie's boyfriends had ever treated **her** like that, which was why they were **ex**-boyfriends. In her twenty-five years she had kissed an awful lot of frogs, and she was beginning to fear that she would never find a prince.

Maisie lifted her chin. 'I walked out,' she said. 'A customer groped my bum and the manager didn't like it when I objected.'

Dulcie sighed. 'How did you object? No, don't tell me – you slapped his face. Or did you pour a cup of coffee over his head?'

'In his lap, actually. And it was an iced coffee, not a hot one. I thought it might cool him down.' Maisie sniggered. 'He looked like he had wet himself. I got a round of applause from the women at the next table.'

'So now you want to stay here, on the farm?'

'Can I? Please?' Maisie hated begging, but she couldn't face going home. She would have to go eventually of course, but not just yet.

Another sigh from Dulcie. 'Give me ten minutes. And Maisie? You'd better tell Mum where you are – I don't want her calling me in a panic.'

Mindful that she didn't want to get her sister's back up any more than she already had, Maisie sent Mum a quick message.

Gone to visit Dulcie for a few days. Wanted to see the goats. Arrived safe xxx

Her mum's reply was short. **Nice of you to let me know.**

At least Mum knew where she was, so she wouldn't worry. No more than usual, that is.

Maisie spied Dulcie's car and waved, wincing when it screeched to a halt. From the way Dulcie was driving, Maisie gathered that her sister wasn't in the best of moods.

'Get in,' Dulcie ordered, making no move to get out and help Maisie heave her case into the hatchback's small boot. 'Planning on staying long?' she asked when Maisie slipped into the passenger seat.

Maisie shrugged.

'Is that a yes shrug, or a no shrug?'

'Dunno.'

Before Dulcie pulled away from the kerb, she uttered a loud sigh. 'Out with it – why are you here?'

To her dismay, Maisie's eyes filled with tears. 'I'm sorry, I should have asked first.'

'Yes, you should have.'

Maisie brushed her tears away. 'Don't worry, I'll leave tomorrow.'

Dulcie softened. 'You don't have to, but I'm warning you, if you intend to stay more than a day or two, I expect you to pull your weight.'

'I will,' Maisie agreed with relief.

'There are the goats to see to for a start, and maybe Otto could use a hand in the restaurant.'

'I'll do anything,' Maisie said, even though she didn't like working in restaurants, pubs or bars. Her previous two jobs had been in pubs. Neither of them had ended well. Maisie suspected she wasn't cut out to be customer-facing. She was, however, looking forward to helping with the goats. They were so darned cute, especially the pygmy ones.

'Have any of them had their babies yet?' she asked as Dulcie eased the car into the road.

'They are due any day now.'

Maisie clapped her hands and let out a squeal. 'I can't wait to cuddle a goatling.'

A smile spread across her sister's face. 'Neither can I. If my goat milk business takes off, there will be plenty more baby goats on the farm. Eventually I'm hoping to be able to give up the day job.'

Oh, yes; Maisie had forgotten that Dulcie had a job, besides running the farm. She worked from home though, so it couldn't be too bad. Maisie would love to be able to work from home, but although she had applied for a couple of jobs where that was an option, she had never even got as far as the interview stage.

'I've got a chap coming tomorrow to give me a quote for converting one of the outbuildings into a pasteurisation shed,' Dulcie was saying. 'I managed to buy the equipment second hand, but I've got to get someone to install it.'

As Dulcie chattered away, Maisie relaxed into her seat. It seemed that her sister had forgiven her for turning up out of the blue. Now all Maisie had to do was make herself useful, so Dulcie didn't send her back home before she was ready to go.

Adam straightened up, wiping his filthy hands on an oily rag, and surveyed the tractor's engine.

'Is it fixed?' the ruddy-faced man in his fifties asked.

'Try it.'

The farmer hoisted his sturdy frame into the cab, grinning when the engine started first time. 'You've done a tidy job.'

Adam dipped his head in acknowledgement; he always did a tidy job and because of that his reputation of being able to fix things was growing. It wasn't just tractors he repaired – he was happy to turn his hand to anything mechanical.

'How much do I owe you?' the farmer asked.

Adam gave him a figure, then as the man went to fetch the money, he began stowing his tools in the van.

'Here you go.' The farmer pressed the money into his hand and Adam wrote out a receipt.

'You've got my number if she gives you any more trouble,' he said, jerking his head at the old tractor. It had seen better days, but with a little TLC and some careful handling, it would last a few more years.

Adam was thankful that this was his last job of the day. He needed a shower, some food, and maybe a pint or two if he could summon the energy to pop along to The Black Horse.

Or he could slump on the sofa with a cup of tea and do his monthly trawl of the internet for properties for sale.

There was nothing wrong with where he currently lived, but he was fast outgrowing the workshop beneath the flat. It was bursting at the seams, and even if it hadn't been, he was ready for a change. He was looking for a place to take his business to the next level. And by buying a more substantial property, he was hoping to make his parents realise that he was serious about it.

His parents didn't like what he did for a living, but that was fine: they didn't need to. What they **did** need to do, was to stop giving him grief about it.

As soon as he arrived home, Adam stripped off and hopped in the shower. Turning the dial up so the water was as hot as he could stand it, he freed his hair from the topknot he wore when he was working, and dug his fingers into his scalp. He had a tendency to wear it too tight and the relief when he took it out was blissful.

A good soaping later and with the water in the bottom of the tray finally running clear, Adam stepped out and towelled himself down before taking a clean pair of joggers out of the drawer, along with a fresh tee shirt.

As well as disapproving of what he did for a living, his parents weren't keen on his flat, either. Or the way he looked. When he had started to wear his hair longer at uni, they had put it down to teenage rebellion. The tattoos (of which he had several) and the eyebrow piercing, they had put down to him wanting to fit in and the influence of the other students. But after he'd finished his course and had continued to refuse to cut his shoulder-length hair or take the silver ring out of his eyebrow, they had come to the conclusion that he was simply being bloody-minded. And the pointed scowls when his tattoos were on display, seriously tried his patience.

It didn't stop him loving his mum and dad though, even if they did exasperate the hell out of him.

As he fried his steak and chopped some salad, he realised it had been a couple of weeks since he'd last seen them, and he vowed to call in soon, before his mum phoned and demanded his presence.

Maybe he would drop in tomorrow. Which reminded him, he had promised to pop up to the farm on Muddypuddle Lane in the morning to give the owner, Dulcie Fairfax, a quote for installing a pasteurisation unit.

It wasn't something he had done before, but he was confident that he would be able to work it out. For some inexplicable reason he had an affinity with anything mechanical: god knows where he got it from, but it certainly wasn't from his dad.

Deciding he was too tired to go to the pub, after he had eaten Adam settled down on the sofa with his laptop on his knees and a cup of tea on the table next to him. Perhaps he would go to the pub tomorrow evening, instead...

Maisie couldn't sleep. It was too quiet. She was used to the noise of the city, even if she did live in the suburbs. The silence here was unnerving, and she had forgotten that it had taken her a few nights to get used to it when she and Mum had visited the farm the previous Christmas.

Maisie wished the inside of her head was as quiet as the outside. Her thoughts were whirling, the events of the past few days praying on her mind. She had been determined not to lose her latest job, but who in their right mind would put up with that kind of behaviour from the punters? She could have had the bloke done for assault, but she hadn't wanted the hassle. It had been easier to take matters into her own hands. The downside was that she had thought it best to resign before she was sacked.

In a moment of indecision, she wondered what she hoped to achieve by coming to the farm. It was safe to say that her job prospects would be seriously curtailed in a small village like Picklewick. She would have been better off staying in Birmingham. But she'd had to get away, unable to face her mother's continued dismay.

Despite Mum fighting Maisie's corner if anyone criticised her, Maisie could tell that she was a disappointment, and she knew Mum must be comparing her to Maisie's siblings. Dulcie had the farm (the lucky cow), Nikki was a teacher, and Jay used to travel all over the world with his job until he'd settled in New Zealand. Also, all three were in steady relationships.

Maisie's defence was that she was still young. At twenty-five, she had plenty of time to decide what she wanted to be when she grew up. And so what if she played the field? Better that, than get hitched to the wrong guy. The problem was, she was beginning to think there weren't any **right** guys out there.

The quiet of the night was broken by the sound of a vehicle coming up the lane and she heard the engine noise change as it putted into the farmyard. Guessing Otto was home and that Dulcie had waited up for him, Maisie thought she'd give her sister a few minutes to tell him they had a houseguest, before going to say hello. She would have a glass of milk while she was at it, and maybe Otto had brought some goodies back with him from the restaurant. She could do with a snack.

After watching a couple of YouTube videos on her phone, she decided enough time had elapsed, so she stuffed her feet into fluffy slippers, wrapped herself up in her dressing gown and padded across the landing. Treading carefully down the steep narrow staircase, Maisie had just reached the bottom step when she heard voices coming from the kitchen.

Hearing her name mentioned, she paused.

Dulcie was saying, 'I don't think Maisie will ever grow up. She drifts through life without a care in the world, taking no responsibility for her actions. I was never like that when I was her age.'

Otto chuckled. 'You're not that much older than her. There are only three years between you.'

'Exactly! That's what I'm saying! Look, you don't have to give her any shifts in the restaurant; I shouldn't have asked. She's likely to do something silly, or decide it's too much like hard work, or whatever reason she gives for packing a job in. And even if she doesn't walk out, employers soon let her go. She's had more jobs than I've had hot dinners. I think she's waiting for the perfect job to land in her lap, but that's not likely to happen. Nikki calls her Maisie Daydream.'

Maisie bit her lip and her eyes filled with tears. That was so unfair. She wasn't **waiting** for the perfect job – she was **trying to find it**. There was a difference.

Otto said, 'I don't mind giving her a chance, if you don't. She can have a couple of shifts and we'll see how she goes.'

'If she tips coffee in any of your customer's laps, she'll have me to answer to,' Dulcie growled.

Otto's laugh sounded too close for comfort and Maisie had the awful suspicion he was immediately on the other side of the door. It was confirmed when he said, 'I'll just get changed, then we'll have a cup of tea before bed, eh? Maybe, with Maisie here, she could see to the animals in the mornings, so you don't have to get up early. We could have a lie-in, for a change.'

The doorknob twisted and Maisie panicked. Instead of pretending to have just this second come downstairs in order for Otto not to realise she had been eavesdropping, she darted towards the front door and was through it in a trice.

Closing it behind her as softly as she could, she tiptoed around the back of the farmhouse and made her way to the barn. Hopefully the goats wouldn't be as judgemental as her sister.

Adam checked the time and realised he had fifty minutes before he needed to be at the farm on Muddypuddle Lane; enough time to stop off in the village for a brunch panini and a coffee.

He eyed the sit-on lawnmower with satisfaction. It was now running as sweet as a nut, and he had even sharpened the cutting blades. It hadn't been part of the repair, but it hadn't taken long with the grinder, and being willing to go that extra mile was helping to build his reputation because the vast majority of work that came his way was by word of mouth.

He lived on the outskirts of Picklewick, in a flat above what had once been an MOT garage, and the farm was in the opposite direction, so he drove through the village, found a parking space on the high street and hopped out, aiming for the cafe a short distance up the road.

'Adam, what can I get you?' Lou asked. She had owned the cafe for years and, in Adam's opinion, served the best coffee for miles.

'I've just about got time for a ham and cheese panini and an Americano, please.'

She flicked a cloth over the counter. 'Find a table and I'll bring it over. Can I tempt you with a slice of strawberry and vanilla sponge?'

Adam's mouth watered. He was a sucker for cakes. 'Go on, but if I can't fit into my jeans, I'll blame you.'

'Pah! It'll take more than one slice of cake! You haven't got an ounce of fat on you. If I was ten years younger...'

Adam sat down, grinning. Lou was an outrageous flirt, but she was like that with all the men, not just him.

'Here, get that inside you,' she instructed, putting his food and a coffee on the table. He noticed she had given him a generous slice of cake, and he reminded himself to leave her an equally generous tip.

As he ate, he scrolled through his emails, glad to see that a part he had ordered for a trailer had been dispatched, and he highlighted it. As soon as it arrived, he would let his customer know and hopefully he would be able to crack on with the job.

Finishing his food, he drank the last of the coffee and settled the bill.

'See you soon,' Lou called, and Adam waved as he stepped into the street. He was a regular at the cafe, calling in two to three times a week. It was more convenient than making his own sandwiches, and it forced him to take a proper break, otherwise he would be eating his lunch on the run.

Suitably fuelled up, he returned to the van. It was time to take a look at Dulcie Fairfax's pasteurisation unit.

The farm was roughly a five-minute drive out of Picklewick, at the top of a steep lane. He used to go up that way a lot when he was a kid, because halfway up the hill was a riding stable, where his mum used to take him for lessons. He quite liked horses, although he hadn't ridden in years. At the time, the farm had been owned by an old chap called Walter York, but he'd moved into a cottage further down the lane, and Dulcie Fairfax lived at the farm now, along with Walter's son, Otto, who had recently opened a restaurant in the village.

Adam had heard that the food in The Wild Side was good, although he hadn't tried it himself and he probably wouldn't any time soon. It was the kind of place you went to for a special occasion, or if you wanted to impress a date. As far as Adam was aware, there were no special occasions on the horizon and he hadn't had a date in ages. Nor did he want one: he wanted to concentrate on growing his business before he allowed himself to become distracted by a girlfriend.

He was still thinking about the stables and wondering whether the place had changed, when he made the right-hand turn on the lane. Over the tops of the hedges he could glimpse horses grazing in the fields to either side, and out of the corner of his eye Adam thought he could see a donkey. There was something incredibly cute about donkeys, he mused.

Easing around a bend in the lane, he changed down a gear as the incline steepened, but as he came out of it, he swore loudly.

Tearing down the road at break-neck speed was a bloody goat!

Adam slammed on the brakes and came to a standstill just as the goat swerved into the verge to avoid his van, and as he did so he realised a woman was racing headlong after it, her arms windmilling as she fought to maintain her balance and not let her feet run away with her.

'What the hell?' he shouted, throwing his hands up in the air. What on earth was she thinking? He had almost ploughed into her. Thank goodness he had been doing no more than twenty miles per hour, if that.

Her horrified expression as she skidded past the van, told him she realised how close she had come to being flattened. But she didn't stop, and his last sight of her was in his side mirror as she carried on running down the lane in hot pursuit of the goat.

Shaken, Adam sat there for a minute, adrenalin from the near miss making his fingers tingle and his heart pound. His good mood gone, he finally pulled himself together and carried on up the hill to the farm, muttering darkly.

Maisie's heart was in her mouth as she spotted Princess, and she slowed to a walk, not wanting to spook her. The goat was calmly munching on something in the hedgerow, but she was perilously close to where the lane met the main road. It wasn't a particularly busy road, but all it took was one vehicle... A van coming up the lane had nearly taken the goat out as it was, but thankfully it had been travelling quite slowly. Traffic on the main road would be going considerably faster.

'There's a good girl,' Maisie crooned breathlessly, as she drew closer to the animal.

Princess carried on munching, but one eye was on Maisie who fully expected the goat to bolt at any second.

Changing tactics, Maisie calmly sidled to the opposite side of the lane, hoping she was conveying total disinterest in the naughty creature.

Whistling tunelessly (it was more of a wheeze than a whistle because she was still out of breath from her mad run down the lane), Maisie put her hands behind her back, lifted her chin, and pretended to be interested in the sky as she strolled nonchalantly past.

Still chewing, a bunch of greenery protruding from one side of her mouth, Princess kept tabs on her progress, and when Maisie reached the point where she was between the goat and the road, Maisie heaved a sigh of relief. Then she let the daft creature have it with both barrels.

Shrieking at the top of her voice, Maisie leapt up and down, waving her arms.

Spooked, Princess uttered a loud bleat, spun to the left and began to gallop back up the lane, her short fluffy tail held aloft.

Maisie, hopeful that the goat would keep heading in the right direction and praying that she wouldn't double back and try to slip past her, followed at a more sedate pace. Now that the immediate crisis had been averted, she felt a bit wobbly. How could she have told Dulcie that one of the goats – and not even **her** goat, because it belonged to Petra at the stables – had escaped? And even worse, that it had been flattened by a car.

Oh, gosh, the look on that van driver's face! All Maisie could remember was a pair of horrified eyes and a wide-open mouth. He had yelled something, but the window had been up, so she hadn't caught what he'd said. Which was probably a good thing, because she had a feeling it wasn't complementary. He had waved his hands in the air, too. He hadn't been very happy with her, and she hoped she wouldn't see him again.

Praying he had business at the stables or Walter's cottage, Maisie was dismayed when she didn't see his van outside either property. She did, however, see Princess, who had paused to continue her lunch and had her furry head buried in the hedge next to the entrance to the farm.

Maisie caught up with her, and with another shriek and more arm-waving, she managed to herd the goat into the farmyard.

Thank god for that, she thought, as she watched the errant creature trot calmly into the barn. But Maisie's relief was short-lived when she noticed the white van parked in the middle of the yard, and saw that its driver was deep in conversation with Dulcie.

Oh, dear, now she was for it!

CHAPTER TWO

As one, Dulcie and the stranger turned to look at Maisie. Dulcie's expression was one of mild bewilderment. The man's expression was furious.

'I could have killed you!' he yelled.

Maisie blinked at his anger. 'There's no need to exaggerate,' she said, walking towards him. Dulcie was staring at her, a frown marring her brow.

'You came tearing down the lane too damned fast,' he cried.

'You shouldn't have been driving up it so fast,' she countered.

'What's going on?' Dulcie's gaze flickered between Maisie and the annoying van driver.

Even as she was arguing with him, Maisie could see how hot he was. Dark hair in a bun on the top of his head, a piercing, tattoos, buff, and the sort of face that belonged on a film star, not a bloody delivery driver.

'I almost ran her over,' he said, just as Maisie cried, 'He nearly mowed me down.'

'What were you—?' Dulcie began, then her frown cleared. 'Princess?'

'Yes, I found her in the barn this morning when I went to feed the goats. I think she expected to be fed, too.'

Dulcie rolled her eyes. 'That goat should have been called Houdini.' She turned to the van driver. 'She's forever getting out.'

'You should take better care to ensure she doesn't,' he retorted. 'This one,' he jerked his chin at Maisie, 'almost got herself killed chasing after it.'

Dulcie's eyes widened and she opened her mouth to say something, but Maisie got in first. 'It's not **her** goat,' she snapped, 'so stop it with the lecturing. Princess belongs to the stables.'

She scowled at him, her hands on her hips, and satisfaction stole through her when his face blanched.

He rallied quickly. 'I don't care who the goat belongs to, you still nearly got yourself killed.'

Dulcie asked, 'Was it really that bad?'

'No!' Maisie cried.

'Yes,' van-man snapped.

'Which is it?' Dulcie's lips were twitching.

'He's being a drama queen.' Maisie pulled a face at him.

He pulled one back.

Goodness knows how long the standoff would have gone on, if it hadn't been for Dulcie, who lost patience with the pair of them. 'Maisie, please tie Princess up before she does another runner. Adam, shall I show you where I want the unit to go?'

He seemed to shake himself. 'Er, yes, please. Sorry about the misunderstanding.'

'I do take good care of my goats, you know,' Dulcie said, her tone frosty.

Adam winced, and Maisie almost felt sorry for him. But not quite. There had been no need to make a mountain out of a molehill.

Dulcie softened. 'It was an easy mistake to make. After all, you are here to give me a quote on installing my goat milk pasteurisation unit, so it was natural to assume the escaped goat would belong to me.'

Ah, so he wasn't a delivery driver.

Maisie's interest was piqued. If he got the job, he would be working here for a day or so, or however long it took.

She tracked his progress as he followed her sister into the single storey stone-built shed attached to the side of the barn, and sighed when the two of them disappeared from sight. She had better go do as she was asked and tie the blimmin' goat up before it got up to any more mischief, then she would let the others out into the meadow. Even though they were all close to giving birth, Dulcie reckoned that a few hours in the early spring sunshine would do them good.

Adam stifled a groan of embarrassment as he entered a shed next to the barn, close on Dulcie's heels. He had just made a total prat of himself in front of a potential new client. Not only had he shouted at the woman who had been chasing the goats, he had also accused Dulcie of not taking proper care of her animals. He was surprised she hadn't ordered him off her property.

Deciding to take the bull (goat?!) by the horns, he said, 'I'm sorry about...' He jerked his head towards the yard. 'It gave me a bit of a scare, that's all. I hope I didn't get her into any trouble.'

'No more than she's in already. I'm in two minds to send her home.'

Damn it, now he felt awful. 'Please don't sack her because of me. I should have driven a bit slower.' He had been driving slowly enough, but if he had to shoulder the blame so Maisie kept her job, he would.

To his surprise, Dulcie burst out laughing. 'Maisie isn't an employee: she's my sister.'

Oh, great. Could this get any worse? He had yelled at his client's **sister?** Then he had to remind himself that Dulcie wasn't his client yet, and probably wouldn't be after this fiasco.

'What do you think?' Dulcie asked, and Adam scrambled to put his lack of professionalism behind him.

He'd been genning up on the milking and pasteurisation process, and he hoped he sounded knowledgeable when he asked, 'Where are you planning on doing the milking?'

'Next door.' She placed a hand on the rough-hewn stone wall to her right.

'Good, not too much pipework.' He knew enough to understand that the area where the goats were milked should be separate from where the pasteurisation took place. 'Can you show me the unit? And next door?'

'Of course.' Dulcie ushered him back outside and headed for another door.

Adam followed, but as he did so, he scanned the yard.

Maisie was nowhere to be seen.

The twinge of disappointment he felt caught him off-guard.

Ignoring it, he focused on the job at hand, making notes in the leather-bound notepad he carried with him when he was working.

'How soon can you get the quote to me?' Dulcie asked.

'This evening?'

'Brill! I thought I'd have to wait a few days.'

'Do you mind if I take some measurements?'

'The unit will definitely fit,' she said, a small line appearing between her brows.

'I can see that, but I'll need to factor in some additional pipework. When will it be ready for me to install?'

'Um...' Dulcie wrinkled her nose. 'I've got to get someone to board the shed out first, and lay a concrete floor.' Her expression was apologetic. 'I've gone about this all wrong, haven't I? I should have got the place ready first before I called you in, and I also need an electrician and a plumber.'

'I can give you a quote for the building work as well, if you like, but I can't do the electrics.'

'Would you? That would be great. So, if the quote is acceptable, when could you start?'

In his mind Adam ran through the jobs that were already booked in. 'The week after next?' He would have to rearrange some things, but it was doable.

Dulcie seemed pleased. 'In that case, I'll leave you to your tape measure. Right, I'd better take Princess back to the stables.' She gave him a grin. 'Try not to run me over when you go down the lane, eh?'

Adam winced. 'I had better apologise to your sister before I leave. She must think me a right numpty.'

'I doubt it. Knowing her, she had her head in the clouds and wasn't looking where she was going.'

Adam was fairly sure she **had** been looking, but that was a discussion he had no intention of getting into. Whatever the tension was between the sisters, he didn't want any part of it.

He made a few more notes, then popped back to his van for a tape measure and his phone. He would give the builder's merchant in Thornbury a call to price up the battening, the lengths of wood and the other materials he would need if he landed the job, so he would have all the information at his fingertips ready for when he came to price up the quote this evening.

As he passed by the barn, he caught sight of Maisie. She was stroking a tiny goat and didn't see him, and of their own volition his feet slowed as he took a moment to study her.

Her lips were moving and he assumed she was speaking to the goat, who kept nudging her hand with its head; for food, he presumed. The scene was reminiscent of an old painting of a rural idyll, apart from Maisie's modern clothes.

Adam only realised he was staring, and had been doing so for several seconds, when Maisie glanced up and caught him.

Briefly he thought how pretty she was, now that he could see her face full-on without it being all angry and shouty;

then her eyes narrowed and her mouth tightened, and he guessed he was about to be shouted at all over again.

Adam got his apology in first. 'I'm sorry, I overreacted,' he began, taking a few steps towards her.

Maisie scrambled to her feet, dusting the straw from her jeans with little swipes of her palms. She tilted her head.

'You did,' she agreed, 'but apology accepted.' She moved closer, studying him. 'At least you cared. Some drivers wouldn't have given a monkey's butt.'

'There is that,' he agreed. 'Is the goat okay?'

Maisie tutted. '**She** is, **I'm** not. I've never run so fast in my life. Dulcie has taken her home. Are you all done?'

'Not yet.' He pointed at the van. 'I need my tape measure. I've got some measuring up to do.' As he said it, he wanted to kick himself. Why else would he want a tape measure, if not to measure something?

Her lips twitched.

'I'd better go fetch it,' he said.

'And I'd better take this little one to the meadow to join her friends. She doesn't seem keen to go, though. It was only after I had put the others in the field, that I realised she was missing.' She sucked in a breath. 'Please don't tell Dulcie. Princess running off wasn't my fault, but losing Cloud would be.'

'Cloud? Is that what the goat is called? Do they all have names?'

'Of course they do! Goats are people, too.' A blush crept into her cheeks. 'Obviously, they're not **people**, but...' She shook her head. 'Shall we start again? Hi, I'm Maisie, I'm Dulcie's sister.'

Adam grinned. 'Hi, Maisie, I'm Adam and I'm not anyone's brother.'

Eyes twinkling, she said, 'I've got another sister beside Dulcie, and a brother. What's it like being an only child?'

'Challenging. What's it like being one of four?'

'Annoying.'

She paused and seemed to be waiting for him to say something more, but his mind was blank. He couldn't think of a single thing, and when she coughed politely, he realised he was loitering.

'Tape measure,' he muttered to himself. 'I, er, hope to see you again, Maisie.' And with that he hurried to his van, grabbed the tape measure and dashed back to the shed.

Hopefully, he wouldn't see Maisie again before he left – he had made enough of a fool of himself for one day.

'Come on, Cloud, you can't loll around in here all day,' Maisie told the little creature. The goat had found a pile of straw to lie down on and was studiously ignoring her. 'Cloud, stop being so lazy.'

The rotund animal let out a small bleat and stretched out her neck as she lifted her tail, her whole body tensing.

'Aw, big stretch,' Maisie said, expecting the goat to clamber to its feet. Instead, Cloud subsided and seemed to settle down again.

Maisie wondered whether she should fetch a halter and a lead rope, and try to get her to shift that way. Dulcie had warned her that goats had minds of their own. As well as being intelligent, they could also be stubborn.

Cloud uttered another odd little bleat, and once again she stretched out her neck, her torso tensing as she strained.

Abruptly Maisie realised what was happening and she clapped a hand to her mouth to hold in a shriek.

Cloud was in labour! Not only was she in labour, but the birth was imminent. Two tiny hooves could be seen at the animal's rear end, and the rest of the goatling was about to follow.

'Dulcie?' she called, trying not to shout too loud for fear of startling the mum-to-be.

There was no answer, and Maisie guessed Dulcie must be in the house.

With a last look at the goat, Maisie ran out of the barn and across the yard, her voice growing louder as she yelled for her sister. Bursting into the kitchen, she shot through the empty dining room and skidded to a halt at the bottom of the stairs.

'Dulcie!' she screeched. 'Cloud is giving birth. Help!'

The house was still and silent, apart from the ticking of the grandmother clock in the corner.

Drat! Dulcie must still be down at the stables.

Maisie thundered upstairs to grab her phone, her fingers shaking as she stabbed at her sister's number. A ringing coming from the kitchen told her that Dulcie hadn't taken her phone with her, which shouldn't be a surprise considering mobile reception on Muddypuddle Lane was so dire.

She resorted to the landline instead and, after looking up the number for the stables, she waited impatiently for an answer. 'Hello? Is that you, Amos? Is Dulcie there? It's Maisie.'

'Hello, Maisie; how are you? Dulcie's just been telling us that you're visiting for a few days. How—?'

'Sorry to interrupt, Amos. I need Dulcie urgently. One of the goats is in labour.'

'Ah, I see. She's gone down to the bottom field with Petra. I'll send someone to fetch her.'

'Thanks. I've got to go; I might need to boil a kettle and find some towels!'

Maisie high-tailed it back across the yard – and ran straight into Adam, who was coming out of the shed. His chest was a solid wall of muscle and it felt like hitting a brick wall.

His arms came around her as she bounced back and staggered.

'Help,' she panted. 'I need help. Cloud is in labour and I don't know what to do. Dulcie's still at the stables and I'm here on my own and I've never given birth to a baby goat before.' She knew she wasn't making much sense, but she was scared, damn it! Dulcie would never forgive her if something happened to Cloud or her baby, and Maisie wouldn't be able to forgive herself either.

'It's okay,' Adam said, steadying her before letting go.

'It's **not** okay. I haven't got a clue what I'm doing and—' She stopped as a faint high-pitched bleat reached her ears.

'It's lucky the mama goat knows what she's doing then, isn't it?' Adam said and stepped aside.

Cloud was on her feet, busily licking the tiniest, cutest baby goat in the whole world. It was lying in the straw, shaking its little head and bleating, and even as Maisie watched, it attempted to stand, heaving itself up on knobbly legs, to wobble for a precarious second before collapsing back into the straw.

Maisie's eyes filled with tears and she brushed them away, her relief acute.

'Who's a clever girl?' Maisie whispered as she crept closer, not wanting to scare the baby, but itching to cuddle it. Then she froze. Cloud's back was hunched once more, and her neck stretched out. 'Oh God, she's doing it again!' Maisie hissed. 'There's another baby in there. What do I do?'

'The same as you did the first time,' he said.

'But I didn't—' she began, then realised what he meant.

'Cloud seems to be managing just fine on her own.'

'What if she doesn't?'

'We'll deal with that if it happens.' Adam's voice was calm, his tone soothing, and gradually Maisie's heart rate slowed.

He was right. Cloud had coped on her own so far, and the odds were that the goat wouldn't need any help at all. But there was something Maisie wanted to know before she allowed herself to calm down fully. 'Do you know anything about goats?'

'Not much.'

'How about sheep?'

'Can't say that I do.'

'Have you seen a baby animal being born before?'

Adam wrinkled his brow. 'Don't think so.'

Maisie sighed in exasperation. 'So if something **does** go wrong this time, how are you going to deal with it?'

'Me?' He blinked. '**You're** the one in charge of the goats.'

'But you said **we'll deal with it if it happens**!'

'I meant **you**.'

Maisie ignored him. She was too focused on the little feet and the tiny nose emerging into the world.

With a final push from Cloud, the newest member of the farm's herd slithered onto the straw, and Cloud turned around to dry it with her tongue. The baby was very much alive, bleating and shaking its head, its little ears twitching.

Maisie shot Adam a delighted look. His smile was as wide as her own, and she clapped her hands and did a jig.

'Aren't they adorable?' she cried. 'Do you think I can pick that one up?'

The first goatling was balancing on legs that it had little control over, and looking confused, as though it was trying to work out what had just happened. Its mum was busy looking after its sibling, and Maisie felt quite sorry for it.

She moved to within touching distance and knelt down, holding out a hand. The baby goat took a wobbly step and butted its nose against her finger. Carefully, so as not to frighten it, she picked it up and held it against her chest. It was solid and warm, and incredibly soft.

Her heart melted. **If this is what it's like to be in love**, she thought, **then I'm head over heels**.

She had adored the goats from the first time she'd set eyes on them. It had been a few days before Christmas when the breeder had delivered eight of the gorgeous creatures to the farm. They were to form the beginning of Dulcie's herd of dairy goats and Maisie hadn't been able to tear herself away, much to her family's amusement. Her brother's partner, who was an artist, had even painted Maisie with the very same goat who had just given birth, and had given it to her as a Christmas present. It was one of Maisie's most treasured possessions.

Footsteps hurrying across the yard alerted her that Dulcie was back, and Maisie turned to face her sister with a huge smile.

Dulcie wore a worried expression as she entered the barn, but when she spied Cloud and the baby healthy and well, her face lit up. And it positively shone when she saw a second goatling in Maisie's arms.

'Two babies!' she cried. 'How wonderful!' She held her arms out and Maisie placed the tiny goat in them. Dulcie checked it over, then put it down and examined the other. 'They're both girls,' she said happily, then she sat on a bale of straw to watch them take their first, vital drink of milk.

Maisie looked on in wonder, only tearing her gaze away when she felt Adam's eyes on her.

The smile they shared felt almost as special as witnessing the birth of two new lives, and she was glad that he had been by her side and she hadn't had to go it alone – despite his dire lack of knowledge about goats.

Later that evening Adam should have been working out some costings ahead of emailing the quote to Dulcie, but his mind wasn't on his task. Whenever he tried to concentrate, his thoughts would wander, and an image of Maisie's blissful expression as she cuddled the baby goat would hover in front of the screen.

He really had made a prat of himself, hadn't he? But he hoped he had redeemed himself a bit when the goatlings were born. There had been that moment when he and Maisie had shared a look. He wasn't sure what it had meant, but it had felt intimate. Or had he read too much into it? He had a feeling it was wishful thinking on his part, which baffled him as he wasn't interested in getting intimate with her (well, he **was**, because he was a man after all, with a healthy sexual appetite) but considering he didn't want to get involved with anyone right now, getting intimate with Maisie Fairfax wasn't an option.

A thought occurred to him: was her surname Fairfax or was she married? He hadn't noticed a wedding ring, and he scoured his memory for one for several minutes until he gave up. Even if she wasn't wearing a ring on the third finger of her left hand, it didn't mean she wasn't in a relationship.

Crossly, he focused on the spreadsheet, telling himself that none of it mattered because he wasn't interested anyway. A girlfriend would be too much of a distraction right now. When his business was more established, he would start dating again (he didn't intend to remain single forever) but not yet. Unfortunately, the downside of not having a girlfriend was that it increased his mother's efforts to set him up with the daughter of one of her close friends. Mum constantly hoped he would change his mind about Verity.

His father similarly hoped Adam would change his mind about joining the firm.

Both of them continued to be disappointed.

So he told himself to stop thinking about the woman he had met at the farm, and think about the job he was hoping to land. But telling himself that was easier than doing it, and her face continued to dominate his thoughts for the rest of the evening

A white blouse and black trousers or a skirt seemed to be a staple uniform of restaurants everywhere, Maisie mused, as she checked that her blouse was tucked in and that her hair wasn't escaping its ponytail.

She was standing in The Wild Side's kitchen, along with the rest of the serving staff, being briefed ahead of the first diners' arrival this evening. Although Otto owned the restaurant and was the guy with the Michelin star, he didn't do all the cooking. He had underlings for that, and she eyed the white-coated kitchen staff with trepidation, knowing that as the tension ramped up, there was a fair chance someone would get tetchy. She just hoped they didn't get tetchy with **her**. She had walked out of more than one job because someone had lost their rag.

Whilst Otto explained the menu to the front-of-house staff, the kitchen staff were busy cooking, and the most delicious smells permeated the air.

Maisie had first-hand experience of just how good a chef Otto was, and she hoped she would get a taste of the dishes on the menu at some point. The Wild Side's unique selling point was that it served only locally grown and foraged ingredients, and flowers featured heavily, and not just because they looked pretty.

Otto expected his waiting staff to be able to identify the various blooms, in case anyone asked, as well as to be able to explain what the foraged ingredients were.

Maisie was facing a steep learning curve, but one that she was determined to get to grips with, because being allowed to stay on the farm might depend on it.

Thinking of the farm brought an image of the adorable little goat babies into her mind, and she couldn't wait for her shift to end so she could cuddle them. Dulcie had been thrilled with the new additions, and Maisie hoped her sister's good mood would continue when she saw the quote for the pasteurisation shed that the guy, Adam, was supposed to email to her this evening.

Maisie was keeping her fingers crossed that her sister would decide to go with Adam's quote – not because Maisie wanted to see him again, but because she knew that when work started on the shed, Dulcie would need all the help she could get. And Maisie intended to provide that help.

She had only been on the farm a fraction over twenty-four hours, but already she felt less tense and she didn't know whether it was the fresh country air that was responsible for the optimism flaring in her chest, or whether it was something else. All she knew was that she didn't want to go back to Birmingham. She wanted a fresh start, and hopefully the farm was where she could make that happen.

CHAPTER THREE

It was Sunday morning and Otto looked exhausted. Maisie had total respect for how hard he worked and the amount of time and effort he had put into getting the restaurant off the ground. No wonder Dulcie needed help around the farm if Otto was putting all his time and energy into his business

As the three of them tucked into a full English breakfast that Maisie and Dulcie had cooked between them, Maisie wondered if there was anything more she could do to help.

Her opportunity came when Dulcie said to Otto, 'I think we should go with that first bloke who gave us a quote. It was very reasonable and he can start next Monday, which gives us a full week to clear everything out and give it a good clean.'

Otto, who had a mouthful of bacon, nodded, but Maisie noticed his slightly pained expression. Dulcie was focused on her plate and didn't see his dismay. Maisie guessed what was causing it: Otto was playing mentor to a visiting chef from London next week, who would be here to gain experience in sourcing and cooking with foraged ingredients, so Otto would be even more pushed for time than he was currently.

'I can do that,' she offered. Over the past few days she had been trying to make herself as useful as possible, cleaning, doing the laundry, feeding the animals, playing midwife to another set of twin goat babies, as well as doing shifts in the restaurant if Otto needed her. Thankfully, she wasn't working today, so she could devote the whole day to doing whatever Dulcie wanted her to do.

'It's mucky work,' Dulcie told her.

'So? I don't mind getting my hands dirty.'

Dulcie cocked her head to the side. 'No, you don't.' She sounded surprised, which Maisie resented, although she didn't show it.

Maisie had never shied away from hard work. What she **did** shy away from was dumb managers and customers with no manners. She also wasn't particularly keen on being stuck behind a desk, and had managed to lose more than one job because sitting in front of a computer all day had driven her mad with boredom. Then there were those jobs on the factory floors that had been equally as boring but with the addition of loud machinery and not being able to have a wee when she needed one. But her main problem was that she wasn't qualified to do anything in particular – mainly because she didn't know what she wanted to qualify **in**.

In the years since she'd left college with three A-levels and a vague idea that something would present itself, she had tried being a junior in a hairdressing salon, a receptionist in a hotel, a chambermaid (different hotel, she hadn't been able to return to the other one), a care assistant in a nursing home (she had been so upset when one of the residents had passed away that she hadn't been able to face going back), a cleaner (in both an office and a school), a sales assistant in a variety of shops selling everything from shoes (ugh – smelly feet) to jewellery (she hated cleaning silver with a passion), and more pub, bar and restaurant jobs than she could shake a stick at. So, no, hard work didn't scare her. Not being happy or fulfilled, **did**.

'I'll get started after I wash up, shall I?' she suggested, so after she had finished stacking the dishwasher, the pair of them donned old clothes and headed outside.

Maisie wanted to check on the new arrivals on the way.

'You're taking your role as goat herder very seriously,' Dulcie teased, as Maisie picked each new bundle up and checked him or her over.

All four were happy and thriving as far as Maisie could tell, and her heart filled with warmth at the sight of them. 'I'm enjoying it,' she told her sister truthfully. It was the best part of being on the farm.

An hour or so later, Maisie was busy shovelling decades' worth of accumulated rubbish into a wheelbarrow, when Dulcie said, 'Have you decided when you're going back to Birmingham?'

Her spirits sank. 'I was hoping I could stay a bit longer.' She hadn't been here a week yet and already her sister was hinting that it was time she left.

'You can,' Dulcie said cheerfully. 'It's just... Mum was on the phone yesterday evening. I think she's lonely.'

Maisie began to feel guilty at leaving their mum on her own in the house, until

Dulcie added, 'I dunno why, because you were hardly ever in.'

'I was!'

'Only at mealtimes and to change your clothes.'

Maisie propped the shovel against the bare stone wall and put her hands on her hips. 'I know you and Nikki think I treat Mum like a skivvy and the house like a hotel, but **you** try living with her. She wasn't as bad when you were at home and Nikki was just around the corner, but since you left and both of you moved to Picklewick, she's been a nightmare.'

'She's worried about you,'

'Well, she needn't be. I'm fine.'

'Are you?'

Maisie softened. 'I'm okay,' she said. 'But I need some time away to think about what I want to do with my life.'

'Have you come up with anything?'

'Not really, although I do like working with animals.'

Dulcie smiled. 'I can see that.'

'Maybe I could train to be a veterinary nurse or a dog groomer.'

'Two rather different professions. But at least you're narrowing it down.'

'How about if I work in a kennels? Or a cattery? A wildlife sanctuary?'

'I'm sure there are plenty of jobs in those areas if you look.'

'In the centre of Birmingham?'

'Probably not.'

'Are there any around here?'

'I'm not sure.' Dulcie sounded hesitant, and Maisie assumed it was because if she did manage to get a job locally, Dulcie would never be rid of her.

'I could open one of my own,' Maisie said.

'A **wildlife sanctuary**?' Her sister's face was incredulous. 'You don't know the first thing about wildlife.'

'I could learn,' Maisie retorted. 'Okay then, what about a boarding kennel?'

'Have you ever looked after a dog? Taken one for a walk?'

Maisie knew she was trying to run before she could walk, but wasn't that where ambition began? People had a dream, then moved heaven and earth to make it come true, and although the dream might be big, the start was small. In order for her to start her career journey, Maisie had to know the final destination.

'Anyway,' Dulcie was saying, 'you need loads of money to set up something like a boarding kennel. You've got to have a property, for a start. You can hardly start one in Mum's garden – it's only big enough for a couple of planters and a patio table. Besides, the neighbours would complain.'

'I know **that,** I'm not stupid.' Maisie gave an exasperated sigh. She wished her family would stop treating her like a kid. 'I would need somewhere like the old farmhouse on the mountain. You know the one, where Jay and Eliza met.' She paused, thinking furiously. 'Doesn't that belong to the farm?'

'Yes, but not for much longer, so you can get that idea out of your head. I'm selling it.'

'Why? It's lovely.'

'It's derelict.'

'It's romantic.' So what if it lacked a roof and had a tree growing in the middle? It would take a bit of work to restore it, but it would look lovely when it was done.

'I have to sell it to pay for this lot,' Dulcie said, gesturing around the shed.

'I thought you said Adam's quote was good?'

'It is, but even so, it's not cheap. Some of the money from selling the old farmhouse will replenish the savings I'll have to dip into to get the pasteurisation shed up and running.'

Maisie experienced a flash of disappointment. She knew it was a pie-in-the-sky idea, but for a minute she had got carried away with thoughts of living there herself and opening a boarding kennel. Or a cattery, or herding goats, or **something**.

The longer Maisie spent at the farm, the more certain she became that she didn't want to return to her old life in the city. The problem was, she didn't have a clue what she was going to do instead.

Whenever Adam drove through the gates separating his parents' property from the secluded lane leading to it, his heart sank, quickly followed by shame that he felt this way. Most people would give their right arm to have grown up in a place like this, with all the privileges that went with being able to afford a house of this size. It was equivalent to a small mansion, complete with winding gravelled drive, sprawling grounds and several outbuildings, one of which housed his dad's impressive collection of eleven classic cars.

Adam drew his van up alongside his dad's Bently, well aware that it would annoy the pants off his old man. His mum would also wince when she saw it, but as her request to park it around the back had fallen on deaf ears up to now, she probably wouldn't say anything since it would only be the three of them for lunch – as far as he knew. He hoped no one else had been invited. Adam didn't think he could face it.

Although Cedar Trees was his childhood home, he had no emotional attachment to the place. Maybe because it was more like a show house than a home. It was beautifully decorated, tastefully furnished and, as far as Adam was concerned, totally lacking in warmth.

He didn't bother to knock or ring the bell, instead walking straight in and calling, 'Mum? Dad?'

'In here,' his mother shouted from the kitchen, and when he followed her voice he found her basting a substantial leg of lamb with its own juices. The aroma of rosemary hung in the air to accompany the smell of roast meat.

She tilted her cheek for a kiss, and he dutifully gave her a peck.

'When will it be ready?' he asked.

His mum tutted. 'Half an hour. Can you wait that long?' Her sharp comment was justified: he had a habit of eating, then dashing off.

But perhaps he wouldn't if his father wasn't so intent on dissing his lifestyle choices and trying to shove his own in Adam's face. Maybe Dad hoped to wear him down, and that Adam would give in eventually. If that was the case, Dad was wasting his time and his breath.

Adam didn't rise to his mum's comment. Instead, he asked, 'Where's Dad?'

'Take a guess – he's in his study, working as usual. He has to, since everything is on his shoulders.'

See, they've started already, Adam said to himself, the inference being that if Adam hadn't stubbornly refused to join his dad's management accountancy firm, then his dad would have had someone with whom to share the burden.

Adam let it go. He had discovered early on that there was no point taking any notice of the barbed comments. It would only cause an atmosphere and he wanted to enjoy his lunch. His mother was an excellent cook (although she often got caterers in) and she took pride in her dinner parties. Which was lucky, since his parents seemed to throw a lot of them.

She asked, 'So, what have you been up to since we last saw you? How long has it been... two weeks? Three?'

'Two.'

'It seems longer. Well, do you have any news?'

He did, but his mum wouldn't be too keen on hearing it. 'I'm doing a renovation on a feed shed up at the farm on Muddypuddle Lane.'

'A renovation? But you're not a builder.'

'No, but it's part and parcel of installing a pasteurisation unit. Goat's milk,' he added, in case she was interested.

She wasn't. She was staring at his hands. No matter how thoroughly he scrubbed them, traces of oil lingered in the creases and under his nails.

'I wish you would—' she began, then stopped and clamped her lips firmly shut.

Adam held back a sigh with difficulty. He must be such a disappointment to them. This life wasn't the one they had envisaged for him, and neither did he look like an accountant. He wondered if they still explained away his hair, piercing and tattoos as youthful exuberance, or had decided he was too old for such an excuse.

He caught his mother staring at his feet, her face full of disapproval. 'Did you have to wear your work boots?' she asked, her brow creasing in displeasure.

'They're not work boots, they're hiking boots. I'm going for a walk after lunch.'

'On your own?'

'Yes, as it happens.'

'You might ask Verity if she would like to accompany you.'

'Not today. Maybe another time.'

Maybe never. Not only did he think that Verity wouldn't be keen on marching to the top of a mountain, he wanted to take a look at the derelict building on his own. He had spotted the listing online yesterday as he had been checking properties for sale. And because he knew where it was and knew he could look around it without involving the estate agent, he thought he would take a gander later this afternoon.

On paper, it seemed to be exactly what he was looking for, and despite telling himself not to get his hopes up, a quiet excitement bubbled in his chest.

Mild irritation had transformed into downright annoyance by the time Adam drove away from his parents' house, and he hoped a brisk walk in the spring sunshine would blow it away.

How much longer would they keep this up? As his mother constantly told him, she couldn't understand why he lived in a (her word) **hovel**, when he could live in luxury at home. Failing that, his parents had offered to buy him a 'nice' house, instead of the 'horrid' flat he currently lived in.

Obviously, Dad would be able to offset it against tax, but that didn't negate the generosity of the offer.

Unfortunately, the offer came with strings, ones which Adam wasn't prepared to have attached to him. He was managing just fine without their help – more than managing, he was doing well. And it was all down to his own hard work and effort. The situation might have been different if he enjoyed number crunching, as he probably would have gone into his father's business. But he hated it. He had only done an accountancy degree because he had felt pressured into it.

At eighteen, he hadn't felt able to escape his father's expectations.

At twenty-one, he had.

His father had railed and ranted for a while, but Mum had convinced Dad that Adam was just going through a rebellious phase, and that he would soon grow out of it.

Seven years later, they were still waiting and their patience was wearing thin. But they failed to see that the more they pressured him, the more determined he was to make a go of his business.

Adam parked the van at the top of Muddypuddle Lane, just above the entrance to the farmyard where the rough tarmacked road turned into an even rougher dirt track.

He got out and stretched, taking a deep breath of clean fresh air as he scanned his surroundings. Properties didn't often come up for sale in Picklewick, and commercial or agricultural ones even less so, which was why he was considering the old farmhouse. It wasn't ideal: from what he could recall, it was more ruin than house and would probably need to be pulled down, despite the best efforts of the estate agent to make the online photos look rustic and charming.

As he strode up the track, which was a public right of way onto the mountain, Adam realised that the surface would have to be re-laid if he wanted to be able to drive his van up it. A tractor could manage it, or an SUV, but not his poor old van. The abandoned farmhouse was also further up the mountain than he remembered, and he was breathing heavily by the time he had tramped up the steep hill and the incline finally levelled off.

Pausing for a moment, he turned around to take in the view.

Waking up to this every morning might be worth the expense of making the old farmhouse habitable. If he was Dulcie, there was no way he would want to sell it. But then again, she already had a similar view.

As he resumed his walk, his thoughts remained on the farm. But it wasn't Dulcie he was thinking of now – it was her sister. Her pretty, vivacious, captivating sister.

Was that Adam's van? Maisie pulled the bedroom curtain aside and craned her neck.

It looked like it, but without a logo or any writing all white vans looked the same. And if it **was** Adam's, surely he would have parked it in the yard and not at the top of the lane?

It probably belonged to a hiker she decided, and her gaze drifted up the hillside, following the path. A solitary man was plodding up the hill and her heart gave a leap. It looked like Adam. Possibly. It was difficult to tell from the back, and he was quite far away too.

But when the figure stopped and turned around, she was sure. It **was** him. She was certain of it. And he appeared to be looking directly at her.

Maisie shrank back, hiding behind the curtain. What was he doing up there? It couldn't possibly have anything to do with the pasteurisation shed, could it?

She decided to find out.

After taking the stairs two at a time, she raced through the dining room, into the kitchen, and shot into the utility room. Stuffing her feet into her sturdy boots, she tied the laces, grabbed her jacket off the hook by the door and dashed outside.

And soon realised her mistake.

At the rate she was walking up the track, she would never catch up with Adam. She might, however, meet him as he was coming back down, but if she didn't want to look silly, she would have to carry on going up the hill. Therefore, she reasoned, it would be better to wait for him to return to his van. If she loitered around the barn, she hopefully wouldn't miss him.

So loiter she did; although it was a good hour and a half before she spotted him coming down the track.

Maisie had her story prepared, and just as he reached his van she sauntered out of the yard and into the lane. Feigning surprise, she did a double-take. 'Hello! Have you come to see Dulcie?'

Adam paused, his keys in his hand. 'I've been for a walk.' He jerked his head towards the track.

'Oh, right. Did you go far?'

'To the ruined farmhouse. I'd forgotten how lovely it is up there.'

'You're local, then?'

He nodded. 'I live in the village. The outskirts, actually – above the old MOT garage on the road to Thornbury.'

'Sorry, I'm not from around here.'

'I guessed as much. Your sister's only been at the farm a year, hasn't she?'

'Yes, she has,' Dulcie said, walking across the yard. 'There you are, Maisie! I wondered where you'd got to, then I heard voices. Hi, Adam.' Dulcie sent him a questioning look.

'I hope you don't mind,' he said, 'but I've been for a walk.'

'Not at all,' Dulcie replied. 'It's a public right of way, and even if it wasn't, you're welcome to go for a stroll. I'm glad you're here, so I can tell you in person that you've got the job. Are you still able to start next Monday?'

'Absolutely.' He was beaming and Maisie felt a rush of pleasure, before immediately tamping it down.

She wasn't here to find a boyfriend – she'd had enough of those in the past. She was here to find **herself.**

Dulcie smiled back. 'Brill. See you next week. Maisie, can you round up the chickens? It'll be dark soon and I want them in their coop so we can eat dinner and settle down. Oh, and the goats need fetching in, too.'

Maisie watched her sister amble back to the house.

Adam hadn't moved, but when Dulcie was out of sight, he jangled his keys.

'I'd better go see to the goats,' Maisie said. 'Congratulations, by the way.'

'Thanks. How are the twins doing?'

'Which ones? We've got two sets now, and a single.'

'You have been busy. I'll need to pull my finger out and get that shed done.'

'How long will it take?'

'About a week, give or take. I'm not honestly sure, as I've never done this kind of thing before.'

Maisie was confused. 'I thought installing equipment was your thing?'

'Not really, although I can turn my hand to most things.'

'So if you don't play with pasteurisation units for a living, what do you do?'

'This and that.'

'You sound like a cowboy.' Adam stiffened and Maisie guessed she had offended him. 'Sorry, I didn't mean that the way it sounded,' she backtracked hastily. It was lucky that she wasn't eyeing him up as a potential boyfriend, because after a comment like that she would have blown her chances.

'That's okay. Apology accepted.' He hesitated and Maisie wondered what he was about to say.

Her surprise when he asked her out for a drink, was almost matched by the delight she felt when she accepted.

CHAPTER FOUR

'I can't speak for long, Mum, I'm getting ready to go to work.'

Maisie's mobile was on speaker phone, sitting on the old oak dressing table. She was peering into the age-spotted oval mirror above it and wishing her lashes were longer. It wasn't fair that a man had longer lashes than her. She was referring to Adam: his were thick and dark, a look Maisie's lashes only achieved with the application of two coats of mascara and a lot of wishful thinking.

'Work? What do you mean **work?**'

Maisie pulled a face at the phone, thankful that this wasn't a video call. 'The restaurant. I'm working there.' It was Wednesday evening and her third shift this week was about to begin.

'**Otto's** restaurant? '

'Yes, Mum, Otto's restaurant.'

'Oh, a mercy job! That's kind of him. But you're not being fair to him, are you?'

Maisie ground her teeth together. 'It's not a mercy job. And what do you mean, 'I'm not being fair to him'?'

'You're taking advantage.'

'I am not!'

'What else do you call it? I doubt whether he had a vacancy just as you rocked up. He feels sorry for you.'

'It was Dulcie's idea,' Maisie retorted, then realised she had probably made things worse.

'Your sister isn't doing you any favours. Enabling, that's what it's called. She's enabling you to run away from your problems.'

Maisie's hand jerked and she narrowly missed poking herself in the eye with the mascara wand. 'Bugger!'

'Just because you know I'm right, there's no need to swear at me.'

'I wasn't swearing at you. I was— Never mind.' She took a deep breath. 'I don't have any problems.' Apart from you, she thought. 'My life is just fine, thanks. Actually, it's not **just fine**, it's pretty good.'

'You can't sponge off your sister forever.'

Oh, good grief! 'I'm not sponging. For your information, I'm pulling my weight.'

'Hmm.' There was a brief pause, then Beth changed tack. 'Have you considered Dulcie and Otto in all this? Have you thought about them at all? They've got enough on their plates without babysitting you.'

Maisie slapped the tube of mascara down so hard that it rattled the mirror. 'I do **not** need babysitting. I am perfectly capable of taking care of myself.'

Yet another change of tack. 'And they certainly don't need you hanging around like a spinster at a party.'

'What?' Maisie rolled her eyes. Her mother came out with some odd sayings on times.

Beth carried on, 'They need time alone together, to be a couple. You're bound to be cramping their style. They can't be doing with entertaining you all the time.'

'They don't have to. I can find my own entertainment.'

'What's his name?' It was said with a sigh, and Maisie easily imagined the eyeroll that went with it.

'Adam,' she snapped, without thinking.

Beth let out a snort. 'I might have known there would be a man involved. What does he do?'

'Why the interest?' Her mum had stopped enquiring about Maisie's boyfriends a long time ago. She decided to leave it there. 'Sorry, I've got to go, Mum. My shift starts in half an hour.'

Her mother made one final effort. 'I'm only asking because I care about you and...' She sniffed loudly. 'I miss you. The house is too quiet.'

Maisie relented. She had assumed Mum would appreciate a bit of me-time, and she had also thought that her mum would have been glad not to have to tidy up after her.

Shame stole over her. Since coming to stay with Dulcie, Maisie had made a real effort to behave responsibly: why couldn't she do that at home? In a flash of clarity, she understood the reason Dulcie and Nikki were often so exasperated with her. When she returned to Birmingham, she vowed to be more responsible. If she could do it here, she could do it there.

But despite her mother's thinly veiled attempt to get her to go back home, Maisie wasn't ready to leave just yet. And she didn't know when she would be.

The following evening Maisie skipped downstairs, excitement fluttering in her tummy. Adam would be calling for her any minute and she was looking forward to it.

She found Dulcie in the sitting room, curled on the sofa, watching TV.

Maisie announced, 'I've got the hens in, and the goats are in the barn. I've also emptied the dishwasher and folded the laundry. I'll iron it in the morning.'

'Thanks, Maisie, I—' Dulcie stopped. 'You're all dressed up. Are you going somewhere?'

'I'm having a drink with Adam. That's okay, isn't it?'

Dulcie frowned. 'I suppose. When was this arranged?'

'Sunday,' Maisie mumbled.

'Why haven't you said anything before now?'

Maisie wasn't entirely sure, although she suspected it might be because she guessed that her sister wouldn't approve. When Nikki had spent a couple of weeks on the farm last summer, she had bagged herself a fella and was now living with him in his cottage in Picklewick. Maybe Dulcie thought that if Maisie got her feet even further under the farm's table, she wouldn't want to leave either.

Her mother's words from yesterday flashed into her head, and she realised that she should have told Dulcie about her date sooner; so much for her resolution to behave more responsibly.

'I wasn't sure whether it would go ahead,' she said, aware that her answer was flimsy. Dulcie opened her mouth to reply, but the rumble of an engine saved Maisie's bacon. 'Gotta go. I won't be late!' she cried. 'Bye!' Then she was out of the door and hurrying across the yard.

The van rolled to a halt, and as it came to a stop she opened the passenger door and jumped in. Her heart was thumping and her mouth was dry, but Maisie wasn't sure whether that was due to Dulcie's obvious disapproval, or because she had forgotten just how good-looking Adam was and how much she was attracted to him.

'Hi.' His voice was soft.

'Hi.' Maisie felt unaccountably shy.

'You look lovely.'

'Thank you.'

'I thought we'd go to The Black Horse. Is that okay with you?'

She nodded; she had a suspicion that anywhere with Adam would be okay with her, and as they drove into the village Maisie wondered why she had agreed to go on a date with him, aside from the obvious – his good looks – and that he seemed to be a nice guy. She was flattered he had asked her out, but was going on a date with him a knee-jerk reaction? Although she didn't go out with **every** guy who asked, she often said yes rather than no. Which was probably why few of them tempted her into going on a second one.

She used to be more picky, but after being swayed by a handsome face or a smooth-talking personality and discovering that more often than not there was little substance behind the polished exterior, she had been casting her net a little wider recently. Unfortunately, she still only managed to catch frogs. Either her taste in men was appalling, or there was a distinct lack of 'good ones' out there. Or they were already spoken for.

She had yet to decide whether Adam was a frog or not, but she was dismayed with herself for going out for a drink with the first man who asked her since she had decided to give dating a miss for a while.

Maisie Fairfax, she scolded silently, **you've got no self-control.** But he was gorgeous, and she defied any woman to say otherwise. Anyway, one date was hardly the same as going steady, was it?

Maisie hoped none of these thoughts were reflected in her face, but she worried that they might be, because he didn't say another word to her until he edged the van into a space in the pub's car park.

However, once they were seated and the drinks had been bought, the conversation began to flow.

'Do you still want to know what I do?' he asked when he had taken a sip of his pint.

'Only if you want to tell me. Or I can carry on imagining you lassoing cows.'

'I've never lassoed a cow. A horse yes, but not a cow.'

Maisie raised an eyebrow, encouraging him to expand on the comment.

'I used to go riding at the stables near your sister's farm.'

'Ah, so you know Petra?'

'Not really. She began working there after I'd knocked horse riding on the head.'

'Why did you stop?'

'It wasn't for me. I was more interested in the tractors than the ponies.'

'When you said **this and that**...?'

'If it's got an engine, I'll give it a go.'

'So you're a mechanic?'

'Not as such. I don't just repair vehicles – I like any kind of machines, from a diesel engine to a lathe.'

'Or a pasteurisation unit,' Maisie chuckled. 'How does it work?' Dulcie had explained how goats were milked, and that unlike dairy cows and their calves, baby goats could stay with their mothers and continue to suckle, so Dulcie would still get the milk she needed.

Maisie was fascinated by the whole process, up to and including the products that Dulcie intended to make out of it, and she couldn't wait to give soap-making a go. She couldn't wait to milk her first goat, either. She had a romantic vision of sitting on a low three-legged stool with her head against the goat's flank as creamy milk squirted into a shiny metal pail.

Unfortunately, Adam's description of the milking process, which involved things like vacuum pumps and regulators, blew her vision to smithereens.

'You've done your research,' she observed.

'Did Dulcie send you to test me? Are you going to hold up a scorecard or give me marks out of a hundred?'

'I might, if I knew more than you. I haven't got a clue how you use one of those things.'

'You'll soon get the hang of it.' He sounded confident.

Maisie wished **she** was: not because she didn't think she could operate it, but because she wasn't sure she would still be here when it was ready to use. Dulcie hadn't indicated that she wanted Maisie to leave, but Mum's comments yesterday had sunk their hooks into her and weren't letting go. Was she in danger of outstaying her welcome?

Pushing the worry aside, Maisie made a conscious effort to enjoy this evening. This was the first time she had been off the farm for fun since she'd arrived. All the other times had been for work.

'Have you lived in Picklewick all your life?' she asked, keen to get to know Adam better.

'Kind of. My parents' house is about two miles outside the village. How about you?'

'Birmingham.'

'Do you miss it?'

'I've only been here just over a week.'

He looked surprised. 'I assumed you were a permanent fixture.'

'I'd like to be.' Her reply was wistful. She knew she wouldn't be able to stay on the farm forever, but she wasn't ready to go back home just yet. And that was mostly because of the goats. She simply adored being around them.

'What do you do – aside from delivering baby goats?' he asked.

'I didn't deliver them, if you remember. Cloud did that all by herself.'

'You supervised,' he said. He was regarding her expectantly.

'This and that,' she replied, a twinkle in her eye.

'Cowgirl?'

Maisie chuckled. 'That's probably one of the few jobs I **haven't** tried.' He arched his brows, so she continued, somewhat defensively, 'I haven't decided what I want to be when I grow up.'

'Goat herder?'

'I wish!' Her reply surprised her, and she blinked. 'Actually,' she said thoughtfully, 'that's not a bad idea. But that would mean staying on the farm, and I don't think Dulcie would go for it.'

'Why not?'

Maisie sighed, debating how much she should share with him, because she didn't want to put herself in a bad light. She resorted to, 'It's complicated.'

'Things often are.' His expression was pensive, and she wondered what **he** didn't want to share on a first date.

When he asked her what bands she liked, she realised he was deliberately changing the subject, which suited her fine, and by the end of the evening she knew his tastes in music (wide and varied), his foodie likes and dislikes, and that he preferred psychological thrillers to action films, although he didn't often go to the cinema.

They had many things in common, and by the time Adam drove the van into the yard, Maisie thought that they had really gelled. Not only was he attractive physically, he also had a friendly, likeable personality, especially when he'd had her in fits of giggles at some of the stories he had told.

One in particular (an incident with a mechanical gazebo and a naked matronly woman in a hot tub) had made her cry with laughter. In turn, Adam had appeared to be amused by her anecdotes of downright rude customers, unreasonable line managers, and some of the unexpected tasks she had been asked to perform.

The one that had amused him the most, was being asked to stand on the loo seats in a male toilet to see if there were any hidden drugs above the ceiling tiles. His reaction when she'd told him she had been working in a school at the time and that the toilet in question was for staff only, had been priceless.

The floodlights in the yard came on as the van bumped across the cobbles. Adam left the engine running and she guessed he wasn't expecting an invitation to come inside the house.

'Thanks for this evening, it was fun,' she said, unclipping her seatbelt.

'Do you want to go out again sometime?'

'Yeah, I'd like that.'

'When do you return to Birmingham?'

'I'm not sure. It depends on how long Dulcie lets me stay.'

Adam studied her. 'Do you think she'll send you packing any time soon?'

'I hope not.'

'Me, too.'

She stiffened as he leant across the seat. In the darkness, his eyes glittered with a question and Maisie answered it by leaning towards him and lifting her chin.

The touch of his lips on hers was electrifying. Her pulse soared as a jolt surged through her and her eyes drifted shut as her lips parted.

Aside from his mouth, he didn't touch her, and when he gently ended it, the disembodied kiss left her breathless with longing. She wanted more of where that came from.

'Friday?' His voice was low and gravelly.

'Pardon?' Hers was higher pitched than usual, and breathy.

'I thought we could go to the cinema.'

'I'm working at the restaurant on Friday.'

'Another time?'

'Saturday afternoon? We could see a matinee. I've got a shift in the evening.'

'I haven't been to a matinee since I was a kid.' He was grinning. 'You'd better pick the film, so you can make sure you're back in time for work. There's a cinema in Thornbury.'

'Good idea. I'll message you.' This time when he kissed her, his arms came around her drawing her towards him.

It was awkward and she felt unbalanced, although she didn't want it to end quite as soon as it did.

'Saturday,' he said, releasing her.

She licked her lips, her mouth tingling. 'Saturday,' she echoed.

As she watched him turn the van around, she wondered whether she might have found another reason to stay in Picklewick.

'You're back, then,' Dulcie said, stating the obvious. She was in the kitchen wiping the counters down, when Maisie entered the farmhouse.

'Looks like it.' Maisie managed to refrain from rolling her eyes.

Had Dulcie expected her not to come home this evening? If so, her sister didn't have a very high opinion of Maisie's morals. She may have had a fair few boyfriends over the years, but that didn't mean she had leapt into bed with all of them: she'd only ever had a handful of lovers.

And neither had she kissed all the men she had dated. Many hadn't even made it to the end of the evening before she had made up her mind that it wasn't working.

'How did it go?' Dulcie asked.

'It was good. Adam is a nice guy.'

'I'm sure he is, but...'

'But what?'

'Are you seeing him again?' Dulcie's expression was disapproving, and Maisie immediately went on the defensive.

'What if I am?'

'I don't think you should.'

'Why? Is it because he has got long hair and tattoos? You're such a goody two-shoes.'

Dulcie's boyfriends had always been vanilla and rather boring. Until she'd met Otto. But Otto was in a league of his own, being a celebrity chef, 'n' all.

Dulcie huffed. 'Just because he's got a couple of tattoos and a pierced eyebrow doesn't mean he's a 'bad boy.' Tattoos are ten a penny these days; no one bats an eyelid.'

'If not that, what is it? Because he's an odd-job man? You're channelling Mum.'

'I am not! I'm nothing like Mum.' Dulcie snorted and flung the dishcloth at the sink. It caught on the tap, hanging there.

'That's the sort of thing Mum would say,' Maisie insisted.

'If you'd let me finish... I don't care if Adam has green hair, a tattoo on the end of his nose, and is covered in oil from head to toe. What I care about is that he's starting work on the pasteurisation shed on Monday and I don't want you messing it up.'

'How the hell can I mess it up? He's hardly going to ask me for advice on how to plaster a wall, is he?'

'No, but I know what you're like. You'll flirt and tease, and lead him on, and then when you've had enough you'll dump him and bugger off back to Birmingham, leaving me to sort out your mess. And I could do without him being distracted, thank you very much!'

'So, basically, you're telling me to back off because I'm so irresistible that he'll do a crap job.' Maisie put her hands on her hips and glared at her sister.

Her sister glared back.

Then Dulcie's lips twitched. 'You do know that you're not all that, don't you?'

Maisie's anger melted away. 'You seem to think I am.'

Dulcie sagged against the sink. 'You've got to look at it from my point of view, Maisie. You get through boyfriends faster than Princess escapes from her pen.'

'That's because they all turn out to be frogs.'

'Frogs, eh? Does Adam have froggie tendencies?'

'Not so far.'

'Which means you will be seeing him again.' It was a statement, not a question, and despite her humour of a moment ago, Dulcie didn't sound happy about it.

'Saturday.'

Dulcie pressed her lips together. 'You've got a shift in the restaurant on Saturday, remember?'

'I haven't forgotten. We're going to the cinema in the afternoon.'

'Hmm. Just make sure you're not late for work.'

'I won't be, I promise. And I also promise not to dump him until your shed is finished.'

'That means you'll be staying here for at least another week.'

Maisie's heart sank. 'Is that a problem?' She had been hoping to stay longer than a week: a lot longer.

'Actually, it isn't. You've been very helpful.' Dulcie sounded surprised, which got Maisie's back up a bit, although she did her best to hide it.

'I've tried to be,' she replied mildly.

'Cocoa?' It was a peace offering.

'Hell, no! I'm not eighty. A glass of wine would be nice.' Then she heard Otto's car in the farmyard. 'Or maybe not. I think I'll go to bed.'

Dulcie gave her a knowing look. 'You don't have to.'

Remembering what their mother had said, Maisie shrugged. 'Otto could do without me hanging around. He sees enough of me at the restaurant. I'll just grab that glass of wine and go upstairs. There's a film I want to watch anyway.'

Maisie was heading up the stairs when she heard Otto come in, and she smiled. With Dulcie admitting that Maisie was useful around the farm, and Maisie making herself scarce so Dulcie and Otto could have some time to themselves, Maisie had put two of Mum's arguments to bed. All that was needed now was for Maisie to try to be the best server Otto ever had, and Mum would have no more objections to Maisie being at the farm.

There was still the matter of being guilt-tripped though, but Maisie couldn't do anything about her mum missing her. Maisie was bound to move out of the family home at some point. She couldn't live with her mum forever, and neither did she want to. It was time Maisie grew up, and she was hoping that the farm on Muddypuddle Lane was the place she would do it.

CHAPTER FIVE

Maisie hurried through her chores on Saturday morning. Not that Dulcie had given her any explicit instructions – Maisie had taken it upon herself to do things, such as collecting the freshly laid eggs from the chicken coop and checking the goats over before ushering them into the paddock.

This morning she also cleaned out the coop, in addition to collecting eggs and feeding the hens their daily grain. Mucking out was a stinky job, and she hoped a hot shower would successfully wash away the whiff of chicken poop. Any romantic notions she'd had about farming had gone the same way as her idea of goat milking. Farming was a mucky, smelly business, but she loved it. Although, when Adam arrived to pick her up just before midday on Saturday, she was still surreptitiously sniffing her hands in case there was a vague hint of hen lingering on them.

Maisie climbed into the van with a smile and a 'Hi,' and as soon as she was settled into the passenger seat Adam stretched across and brushed his lips lightly against hers, before putting the van into gear and pulling out of the yard.

'Hi, to you, too,' he said. 'I hope you didn't mind me suggesting a quick bite to eat first, but I thought you mightn't have time to grab anything before you had to go to work.'

Maisie didn't mind at all. She had been pleasantly surprised at his thoughtfulness. In her experience it was a rare commodity. 'Where were you thinking of?'

'Will Mexmax do you? It's next door to the cinema.'

Maisie loved the spicy chicken and huge burgers that the restaurant chain was renowned for, so she was more than happy, and half an hour later the pair of them were seated in a corner booth, perusing the menu.

'Are you sure you want to see a rom com?' she asked, deciding to have a hot and spicy burger with fries, and an ice cream sundae to follow. The film she was referring to was the latest hilarious blockbuster, and although she wanted to see it, she guessed Adam mightn't be as keen. However, her choices had been limited due to the start times and film length, as she had to ensure she was back in Picklewick by six-thirty.

'It sounds like fun,' he replied gallantly, and if she hadn't liked him before, Maisie seriously liked him now.

'Your choice, next time,' she said, then winced as she realised she was assuming a lot.

'Deal. How do you like working at The Wild Side?'

'It's good as far as waitressing goes. I can't see myself doing it long term though, even if Otto is practically family.'

'Ah, yes, goat herding,' Adam teased gently.

'Not just goats. I've also grown quite attached to the chickens, especially Kevin.'

'Kevin?'

'That's my nephew's chicken. She's female but Sammy has named her Kevin. She's incredibly tame. And so is Flossie, the sheep. She was hand-reared by Otto's dad, Walter. He owned the farm before Dulcie.'

'I know.'

Maisie blushed. 'Of course you do, what with you being a local. I keep forgetting that everyone knows everyone else in Picklewick.'

'I don't know everyone **personally,**' he said. 'But I usually know **of** them. When Walter and Otto put the farm into a lottery, it was the talk of the village. I even bought a ticket.'

'You didn't!'

He nodded, smiling his thanks as a server delivered their meals to the table.

'I can't see you owning a farm,' Maisie said, tucking into her burger.

'Neither can I, but I can see me owning all those barns and outbuildings.'

'Why? What would you do with them?'

'Expand my business. I'm quite limited at the moment. I've been looking for something bigger, but there's not much about, especially on my budget.'

He looked wistful, and Maisie felt for him. She would like a place of her own too, but that wasn't going to happen anytime soon.

After the meal was finished, they strolled over to the cinema.

'Where would you like to sit?' Adam asked as they entered the theatre. There were two tiers, one nearer to the screen, which was almost flat, and the other up some shallow, wide steps.

'Not right at the front. We'll get cricked necks.'

'The back row?'

'Like a couple of teenagers?'

'It depends on whether you want to watch the film, or make out.'

Maisie giggled. 'How old are you? Sixteen? How about this one?'

'I'm happy if you are,' he said, and she sidled into the row, aiming for the middle.

By mutual agreement, they had decided not to buy any snacks, both of them still full from the meal, so they settled down to watch the film.

Maisie was soon immersed in the story, however she was also very conscious of the man sitting next to her, and every so often she stole a glance at him out of the corner of her eye.

When his hand reached for hers, a tingle shot through her which made it difficult to concentrate on the film after that. She kept hoping he would kiss her, but he seemed content just to hold her hand.

It wasn't until he was dropping her off at the farm, that he finally made a move.

This time, the kiss lasted longer and was far more satisfying, although it did leave her wanting more.

It was Maisie who ended it, but only because she had to get ready for work. 'I've got to run,' she said. 'I have to be at The Wild Side in forty-five minutes.'

'I can drop you off, if you like. I'll be driving past it on my way home.'

'That's great – if you don't mind. It'll save me walking or asking Dulcie for a lift.' She'd only had to do that once so far, as she usually either went into the village with Otto or she walked along the path through the fields. The one time she'd asked Dulcie for a lift was because it had been raining.

It occurred to Maisie that if she did persuade Dulcie to let her stay for any length of time, she would have to buy herself a little run around; constantly begging Dulcie for lifts would be a sure-fire way of outstaying her welcome. Maisie just about had enough money in her savings account to buy an old banger, and at least she could ask Adam to take a look at it if it packed up.

'Would you like to come in and wait?' she offered, her fingers on the door handle. Adam hesitated. 'Or maybe not, if it will make you feel uncomfortable,' she added.

'I'm starting work on Dulcie's shed on Monday,' he reminded her. 'It mightn't be appropriate.'

'I understand.' Impulsively she leant across to give him a swift kiss. 'I'll be as quick as I can.'

Dulcie, who was in the dining room staring at her laptop when Maisie dashed inside, glanced up with a frown. 'You're cutting it fine. I suppose you want a lift?'

'It's okay, Adam will drop me off at the restaurant.'

'Hmph.'

Irritated, Maisie shot upstairs to change into her work clothes. From her reaction, Dulcie hadn't come around to the idea of Maisie dating Adam, and Maisie felt as though her sister was judging her and finding her wanting.

Even if this afternoon's date had been a disaster, Maisie wouldn't have done or said anything to jeopardise Adam starting work on the pasteurisation shed on Monday. She wasn't that stupid, no matter what her family thought.

'See you later,' she said, as she breezed through the dining room, and she was out of the door before Dulcie had a chance to reply.

'Ready?' Adam asked as she climbed into the van.

Maisie nodded. 'Thanks for this – and for lunch and the cinema.'

'My pleasure. Will you be around on Monday morning?'

'Absolutely! I've got chores to do.'

His smile was warm. 'I'll see you on Monday, then. Maybe we can do something later in the week?'

'I'd like that,' she said, meaning it. And when she gave him a quick kiss in the van outside the restaurant, she knew that Monday wouldn't come quickly enough.

Maisie was up extra early on Monday morning: not because she intended to take greater care with her appearance (there wasn't any point when she would soon have straw in her hair and muck over her clothes) but simply because she was excited to see Adam.

Having managed to spend an inordinate amount of time thinking about him yesterday, she was now restless and on edge at the prospect of seeing him again this morning. By the time he turned up, she was a bundle of nerves and she was forced to give herself a stern talking-to.

Maisie Fairfax, she said to herself, **what on earth has got into you? You are never normally like this with a guy.** Then, as she watched Adam get out of his van from her observation point in the kitchen as she stood near the sink and peered out of the window, it struck her – she was falling for him.

Her startled gasp made Dulcie shoot her a concerned look. 'Are you okay?'

'I'm fine. I stubbed my toe, that's all.'

Dulcie walked over to the sink to rinse out a mug. 'Is that Adam, I see?'

Maisie pretended she hadn't noticed his arrival. 'So it is. He's early.' It was only seven forty-five.

'I'm not complaining,' her sister said. 'The sooner he starts, the sooner I can begin milking the goats. In fact, I think I had better have a go at milking Cloud and Bramble by hand, to get them used to the idea. Want to help?'

'Yes please!' Maisie couldn't think of anything she'd like more.

Can't you? an inner voice piped up, as the memory of Adam's kiss burst into her mind.

Shoving it away – she wasn't here to kiss frogs (or princes) – Maisie followed her sister outside, eager to have a go at milking her very first goat.

Adam was unloading an assortment of tools from his van, but he stopped what he was doing when he noticed her and Dulcie.

'Morning.' He directed the greeting at Dulcie, but his gaze flickered towards Maisie.

'Can I get you a coffee before you start?' Dulcie asked.

'I'm good, thanks. I always bring a flask with me.'

'Okay, but let Maisie know if you need anything, because I'm starting work in an hour. Before that though, we've got a goat to milk. Wish us luck.'

Maisie hoped she wouldn't need any luck; she hoped she would be a natural.

From the ruckus that had been coming from the barn every morning for the past couple of days, Adam assumed that milking goats must take a bit of practice. He was halfway through the renovations to the pasteurisation shed and every day so far this week he'd heard irritated bleating, buckets being overturned and some choice swear words.

He hadn't mentioned anything until now, but this third date with Maisie seemed an ideal opportunity to bring it up. It was Wednesday evening, and they were having a meal in The Black Horse.

'How is the milking going?' he asked.

'Ugh! It's not.' Maisie shuddered.

'I did hear some swearing,' he admitted, 'so I guessed as much.'

'Petra has promised to show Dulcie how it's done tomorrow. Surely it can't be that difficult? And what will happen when we try to milk them mechanically?'

Adam smirked. 'I'm glad it's not my problem. I'll stick to engines, thanks.'

'When will you be finished?'

'Friday, if I don't hit any snags.' He would be sorry the job was ending: seeing Maisie every day had been the highlight. He was hoping to continue to see her after it was over, but he supposed that depended on how much longer she would be in Picklewick. She didn't appear to be in any hurry to return to Birmingham, and she had even indicated that she would like to make the village her permanent home.

The sound of tinny music had Maisie scrabbling around in her bag, and when she saw who was calling, her face fell. 'It's my mum,' she said. 'I'd better take this, sorry.'

Adam didn't mind in the slightest. He was curious about her family, and although he tried not to look as though he was ear-wigging, it was impossible not to hear, considering she was holding the conversion less than a metre away.

'Hi, Mum... No, not tonight, I'm out for a meal... The Black Horse... With Adam... **Adam**. He's installing the past— Not yet... I don't know... I would have thought you'd enjoy not having to tidy up after me. Look, Mum, I've got to go... Love you, too.'

She made sure the call had ended, then sent him an apologetic look. 'Sorry. I wasn't expecting her to phone. I only spoke to her yesterday. She's missing me. I don't know why – she spends most of the time grumbling that I treat the house like a hotel.' Maisie's expression was sheepish. 'She's right: I do. I think the problem is that I've never left home. Why is it that I revert to about sixteen when I'm with her?'

Adam's parents were the same; they didn't seem able to trust his judgement when it came to what he wanted to do with his life.

Maisie continued, 'It doesn't help that I'm the baby of the family. I don't think she likes the idea of her last chick flying the nest.' She sighed. 'She's nagging me to go home, but the longer I'm here, the more like home it's beginning to feel. Except it's not **my** home, it's Dulcie's, and I don't know if she'll put up with me for more than another couple of weeks.'

'Is it Picklewick itself you like, or the farm?'

'Both, but the farm especially. I like working with animals.'

'Aren't there any animal-related jobs in Birmingham?'

'Possibly. Why? Are you trying to get rid of me?'

'Absolutely not.' His reply was emphatic. The thought of her returning to her hometown made him feel rather sad.

'I'm glad.' Her gaze captured his and he was momentarily lost in her eyes.

She broke the spell. 'Fancy another?' Their glasses were empty, as were their plates.

'I'd better have a soft drink,' he said, having already enjoyed a pint with his meal.

'If you want another, I don't mind walking back to the farm,' she offered.

'I am not letting you walk home on your own; it's nearly dark.' He had a thought. 'Would you like to come back to mine for an hour?' And when he noticed her hesitation, he hastily added, 'Just for a coffee, I promise. I might even be able to stretch to a Jaffa cake or a chocolate Hobnob.'

'Now you're talking! Who can resist a chocolate Hobnob?'

Adam smirked. 'I know the way to a woman's heart.'

It struck him as he said it, that he wished he **did** know the way to Maisie's heart, because he abruptly realised that she was beginning to worm her way into his.

Maisie assumed she must have passed Adam's place on the way into and out of the village on several occasions, but she had never given it a second glance. It was a stand-alone building, three stories high, with a set of large garage-type wooden doors dominating the ground floor. They were painted sky-blue, but had seen better days. As had the door next to it, which she assumed led to the living area upstairs. The brickwork was a dingy cream render, and there was a concreted area at the front daubed with oil stains. An old sign above the garage doors said **MOTs HERE** and the outside looked run-down and unloved.

Maisie hoped, for Adam's sake, that the flat was in better nick, and she could understand why he wanted to move but at the same time she was envious that he was able to rent a place of his own. She wished she could afford to.

Far from being dingy, the tiny hall and the stairs leading to the living accommodation above, were clean and bright, with white walls and a wooden staircase. And when Adam showed her into the flat, she was delighted.

It was a bit blokey for her taste, being sparse and lacking in soft furnishings, but it was as neat as a pin (as her mum would say) and was spotlessly clean.

An L-shaped black leather sofa dominated the living room, and a TV hung on the wall opposite. An old-fashioned LP player sat on a rack of industrial-looking shelves, along with a selection of books and a potted plant. A staircase led to the top floor and, she assumed, the bedroom.

The flat was bigger than she had expected, and another twinge of envy twisted in her stomach. Maisie would give her right arm to live in a place like this –

even if it did have a dirty garage-cum-workshop underneath.

'Coffee or tea? Or I've got a bottle of pale ale if you're interested.'

'Coffee, please.' She dropped her bag and jacket on the arm of the sofa and followed him out to the kitchen. This, too, was immaculate: not a dirty mug or a used spoon in sight. 'Are you always this tidy?' she asked.

'Yeah.' He fired up an impressive-looking coffee machine. 'Just because I'm a guy living on my own, doesn't mean I'm a slob.' His wry smile took the sting out of his words.

'I need to take a leaf out of your book,' Maisie muttered. 'I'm the slobby one in my family.'

'I'm sure you're not as bad as that.'

'Oh, I am, believe me. Although, I seem to have turned over a new leaf since coming to Picklewick.'

'Trying to impress Dulcie?'

'You could say that.'

When the drinks were ready they took them into the lounge, but Maisie hadn't managed to take a single sip of hers before Adam slid across the sofa and kissed her.

This was no brief flutter of the lips; this was a passionate, toe-curling, breath-stopping kiss.

The shock of it went right through her before settling deep inside, leaving her trembling with desire. She slowly slid down onto the sofa until she lay on her back, Adam above, holding his weight on one arm until she pulled him down. His body covering hers, her fingers crept underneath his shirt to caress his back, and at her touch he shifted position with a groan and continued to kiss her deeply for several deliciously long minutes.

Maisie wasn't sure how far she would have allowed things to go, but she didn't get the chance to find out.

'Stop, stop,' Adam moaned, dragging his mouth away from hers.

He pushed himself upright and sat back. His hair was tousled, his shirt raised on one side, and he was breathing hard. He looked delectable, and Maisie wanted to eat him whole.

'I'm sorry,' he said, his voice hoarse. 'I got carried away for a moment.'

Maisie adjusted her top and shifted into a sitting position. 'So did I.'

'It was only supposed to be coffee.'

Her smile was small. 'We both knew it was going to be more than that.'

'But I don't want you to think I lured you here under false pretences.'

'I don't. Anyway, I could have stopped you sooner, but I didn't want to.'

He opened his mouth, but whatever he was about to say was lost by the ringing of his phone. 'Dear god,' he muttered. 'I sure know how to kill the mood, don't I?'

'Are you going to answer it?'

He checked the screen. 'It's my mother.'

They exchanged sympathetic glances as he accepted the call.

'Hi, Mum.'

Maisie strained to listen as his mother spoke, but she couldn't hear a thing.

'No, I wasn't in bed,' he said, catching her eye again.

Maisie blushed and Adam quickly looked away. Feeling awkward, she was about to ask where the loo was, when he lowered his phone and mouthed, 'Are you working on Saturday evening?' As she nodded to tell him that she was, Maisie could hear a faint tinny, 'Adam? Adam!' coming from the speaker.

'Hang on, Mum, yes, Saturday is fine, I'll see you then.' Then he did what Maisie herself had done less than an hour previously, and stabbed at the phone, making sure the call had disconnected. 'It looks like I'm going to my parents on Saturday for dinner,' he said. 'At least it'll save me having to cook. I would have preferred to see you, though. When are you free next?'

'Sunday.'

'Fancy doing something?'

Maisie certainly did, but what she **fancied** doing wasn't what she **should** be doing. It was a long time since a man had gotten under her skin the way Adam had, and she knew she had to take it easy.

'We could go into Thornbury and check out a pub or two,' he suggested, and Maisie breathed a sigh of relief.

She wanted to get to know him better first, and even then she mightn't take things to the next level – not if it looked like she would definitely be returning to Birmingham.

Until she knew what was happening, she needed to guard her heart. The last thing she wanted was for it to be broken.

CHAPTER SIX

Adam was in the middle of flushing out the pasteurisation unit ready for its first use, and was currently running his hands along the pipes to check for leaks, paying particular attention to the joints and the valves. Dulcie was hovering anxiously, Maisie by her side. The two of them wore worried expressions.

He sidled past them and went next door to the milking parlour, where he did the same thing. Maisie and Dulcie followed him.

'I need a goat to check it properly,' he said.

He hadn't heard quite as much swearing during these last two days, so he was hoping that the animals were getting used to being milked. However, how they would react to having the business end of the milking machine attached to their udders was a totally different pot of yoghurt.

Maisie said, 'I'll fetch Cloud. She's the most patient.'

Adam also knew that Cloud was one of the pygmy goats and would therefore be easier to handle if the critter decided to take exception.

Maisie was back in a trice, Cloud and her two goatlings in tow.

'Do you want to do the honours?' he asked Dulcie, hoping she didn't expect **him** to try to milk the goat. As far as he was concerned, his job was done as long as the damned thing worked – and he couldn't see any reason why it wouldn't.

He could barely bring himself to watch as Dulcie manoeuvred the goat into position on the raised platform and presented the animal with a hay net filled with vegetable treats to keep it occupied whilst she fiddled around with attaching the suction cups.

Apart from an occasional annoyed stamp of a hoof when Dulcie was too clumsy, the goat didn't seem particularly bothered.

Adam held his breath, almost sagging with relief when creamy milk finally began flowing along the clear tubes. Not that he had thought for one second that he wasn't capable of installing such equipment, but no matter what job he did, there was always an element of worry that something might go wrong.

'Result!' Maisie cried, clapping her hands, and he gave her a triumphant grin. She got her phone out. 'This calls for a selfie,' she said, and she draped an arm around his shoulders and pulled him close, holding her phone aloft.

Their cheeks touching, Maisie took a snap with the goats in the background. Then she insisted on taking a photo of him with Dulcie.

Adam, conscious that his relationship with Dulcie was considerably more formal than his relationship with Maisie, made sure to keep a respectable distance, and he moved out of the way entirely when Maisie started snapping the goat.

Abruptly remembering that he was supposed to be checking the machinery, Adam hurried into the other shed, following the milk's progress, and was relieved to find everything working as it should.

A few minutes later Dulcie joined him, the goat having been successfully milked.

'You've done a good job,' she said. 'I'm really pleased. Come into the house and I'll get your payment sorted.'

'There's no rush.'

'I want to get it out of the way, and I expect you could do with the money.'

He shrugged, not knowing what to say to that. He wasn't exactly destitute, so it could wait a few days, but if Dulcie wanted to settle the debt now, he wouldn't say no.

Maisie was leading a bemused goat out of the milking shed as he emerged into the yard.

'This is a momentous occasion,' she declared, beaming widely. 'We should have an opening ceremony.' The goat bleated, as though in agreement.

'We should have something,' Dulcie agreed. 'But I was thinking more like a goat-petting experience. With the addition of some rabbits and a few chicks, we might encourage visitors to the farm. It's something I thought about last autumn, but I haven't had time to organise it.'

'I'll do it.' Maisie's face was alight. 'Let me, please.'

Dulcie said, 'You just want to get your hands on some fluffy chicks.'

'Yep.' Maisie was totally unashamed.

'We can have a chat about it tomorrow,' Dulcie said. 'Otto will be around in the morning, and I think Sammy wants to see Kevin, so we can pick Nikki's brains at the same time.'

Cloud bleated and tugged on the lead rope, reminding Maisie she was there. 'I'll take her back to the meadow,' she said, then turned to Adam. 'I expect you'll be gone by the time I get back.'

'Probably. Are you still up for Sunday?'

'Absolutely. See ya.'

Adam took a moment to watch her skip across the yard, the goats close behind.

Then he realised Dulcie was staring at him and he looked away.

'Come on.' She gestured for him to follow as she went into the house. 'Will a bank transfer do you?'

'It certainly will. Um, Dulcie, I noticed that the old farmhouse on the top of the hill is up for sale. Have you had much interest?'

'None at all, unfortunately. I suspect it's too remote and too much work needs doing, especially since the access road is so poor.' She pulled a face. 'You can't actually call it a road, it's more like a dirt track. Why? Are you interested?'

'I might be.'

'What would you do with it?'

'Live in it. And put up some outbuildings.'

'What's wrong with where you are now?'

'Too small. Anyway, it was only ever meant to be a stop gap.'

'Do you want to have a look around?'

'I've been up there already. I agree, it will need a tremendous amount of work. But it'll be lovely when it's done.'

Dulcie studied him. 'You'll need deep pockets.'

She was right. Plus he would have to sell his place first to raise the necessary funds. Which meant he would be homeless for a while – unless he moved back in with his mum and dad.

The thought filled him with unease. It had taken a lot of effort to escape from his parents' house and the last thing he wanted was to move back in and have his mum looking over his shoulder every five minutes, telling him what to do and how he should do it. Maybe he could buy a cheap caravan, put it on the site and live there for the duration?

'The payment has gone through,' Dulcie said. 'It should hit your bank account in a few minutes.' She straightened up. 'If you're serious about the old farmhouse, let me know.'

'I will,' he promised. 'But can you keep it just between you and me, for the time being?'

'Of course.' She glanced out of the window and Adam guessed she must be thinking that he didn't want Maisie to know. Which he didn't, but only because he wanted to get everything straight in his head first, before he mentioned it to her. However, the main reason he didn't want anyone to know his business was because if his parents got to hear about it, they would do their utmost to talk him out of it, and he could do without the grief.

The following morning Maisie and Dulcie did the milking between them. It took them fifty minutes to milk five goats.

Maisie said, 'It'll get easier as the goats get used to it.'

Dulcie was looking rather despondent. 'I hope so! I can't do this every morning, I haven't got the time. Thank goodness today is Saturday, otherwise I'd be late starting work.'

'I'll do it,' Maisie promised, adding, 'For as long as you need me to.'

'That could be a couple of weeks,' her sister warned.

Maisie didn't take it as a warning, she took it as a promise. It meant she would have another two weeks on the farm before she was forced to re-evaluate her life. 'That's okay, I'm not in any hurry to go back to Birmingham.'

Maisie realised she had said 'Birmingham' and not 'home' and she wondered whether Dulcie had noticed.

It seemed not, as her sister said, 'Nikki and Sammy will be here soon. Let's put this milk in the fridge, then we can crack on with brainstorming some ideas.'

When they returned to the house they were met by the delicious aroma of baking, and found Otto taking a batch of croissants out of the oven. He'd no sooner done that, than Nikki rocked up with Sammy with his young Border collie at his heels.

'Mum said you've got more baby goats!' he cried. 'Can I go and see them?'

'Of course you can,' his mum said, and four pairs of eyes watched him indulgently as he shot out of the door with a loud whoop, the dog in hot pursuit.

'Let's take a look at this new set-up, then,' Nikki said, just as Walter arrived. He had also brought his dog with him. Peg was a Border collie too, but considerably older and a lot calmer than Sammy's pup.

Maisie held out her hand for the dog to sniff, then fondled Peg's ears. That was what the farm lacked, she thought: a dog. There was an old ginger tom cat who came and went when the mood took him, but the animal belonged to Walter and wasn't the friendliest of creatures.

Whilst Dulcie showed Nikki and Walter the new milking parlour, Maisie stayed put and played with the dog until they breezed back in.

'Adam is a bit of a hottie,' Nikki declared, as Otto placed the croissants in the centre of the table. She took one and bit into it, cupping her hand underneath her chin to catch the crumbs. 'Mmm, this is lovely,' she mumbled around a mouthful of pastry.

'He is,' Maisie acknowledged. She had sent Nikki, Jay and their mum the photos she had taken yesterday.

Nikki furrowed her brow. 'Dulcie mentioned that you two are an item. How long before you dump this one?'

'Who says I'm going to dump him?'

'You always do. Anyway, you'll have to when you go back home.'

Maisie pressed her lips together. She didn't want to think about that right now. Besides, she still had a couple of weeks' grace.

'Good job really,' Nikki carried on. 'Mum wouldn't approve. She hates piercings.'

'And long hair,' Dulcie added.

'She isn't too keen on tattoos either,' Nikki said.

'I've got a tattoo of a sheep,' Walter announced, rolling up his shirt sleeve to show them. Maisie was bemused. If she were to have a tattoo, it certainly wouldn't be a **sheep**.

'Can I have a tattoo?' Sammy piped up. He had returned to the kitchen, catching the tail end of the conversation.

Five adults said in unison, 'No, you can't.'

'I'll have one when I'm grown up,' he said. 'I want a tattoo of a chicken.'

Otto said to his father, 'If Sammy ends up having a chicken on his arm, you know who Beth will blame.'

Walter waved a hand in the air. 'As if I care. It'll be just one more thing that Beth and I don't see eye-to-eye on.'

Maisie recalled how her mum and Walter had squabbled like a pair of kids when the family had spent Christmas at the farm. It had been quite entertaining, with the added bonus that whenever Mum's attention had been on Walter, it hadn't been on her.

Dulcie accepted a cup of coffee from Otto with a smile, then raised her voice. 'Can we get on with ideas for the petting-zoo-spring-event thingy, because Otto has to leave soon.'

'You could have koalas,' Sammy suggested. 'People like koalas.'

'You mean, **you** like koalas,' Nikki pointed out. 'I don't think Aunty Dulcie will be keeping koalas.'

'Uncle Jay could send her some.'

His mother said, 'Koalas are native to Australia, not New Zealand.'

Dulcie sipped her coffee. 'We've got the goats, and three of them have yet to give birth. But that will be soon, so I want to hold the spring event thingy in the next couple of weeks ideally, so the babies are still tiny.'

Otto grinned. 'Spring event thingy? Catchy title.'

'I'm not sure what else to call it,' she said.

'How about Spring on the Farm, or you could hold it at the Easter weekend and call it an Easter Fayre?' Maisie suggested.

'I like that idea! Good thinking, Maisie. Now, how about if we—' Dulcie began, but was interrupted by her phone ringing. 'It's Mum,' she said, accepting the call. 'Hi, Mum. Hang on, let me put you on speakerphone. Just so you know, Maisie,

Otto, Nikki, Sammy and Walter are here, so no swearing.'

'Hi, Mum,' Maisie and Nikki chorused in unison, as the others said hello.

'What are you all doing at Dulcie's at this time on a Saturday morning?' Beth wanted to know.

Dulcie said, 'They're helping me plan the Easter Fayre.'

'What Easter Fayre?'

'The one I intend holding to try to bring in some revenue.'

'I thought that's what the goats were for? And who was that man you were draped over, Maisie? Was that the chap who Dulcie got to do all the work?'

'His name is Adam,' Maisie said.

'He looks a bit of a sort,' Beth replied. 'Is he the one you've been seeing?'

'Yes, he is.' Maisie shook her head in irritation, catching an I-told-you-so look from Nikki.

'You can do better than him,' Beth continued. 'But then, I doubt he'll last long. Your boyfriends never do.' It was said with an equal measure of satisfaction and disapproval. 'I don't know why you can't find yourself a nice chap like Otto. Or Giovanni.'

Nikki rolled her eyes as she muttered, 'It's nice of her to include Gio.'

Maisie smirked at her eldest sister and Nikki stuck out her tongue, making Maisie blink in surprise.

Dulcie frowned at them and held up a hand. 'Mum, is there anything in particular you want? I don't like to be rude, but Otto has to go to work in a minute and I want to get on with the meeting while he's still here.'

There was a telling silence, followed by, 'I know when I'm not wanted, so I'll say goodbye. Clearly Walter's opinion is more important than mine.'

'Don't be silly, Mum. Your opinion is equally valid. I know, why don't you stay on the line? It'll be as if you are actually here.'

'But I'm not, am I? I'm here on my own. Maisie, when are you coming home?'

Dulcie tutted, 'Mum, can we get on, please? Do you want to stay on the phone or not?'

'I suppose I'll have to, if I want to be part of the family.'

Maisie wrinkled her nose as her sisters pulled equally irritated faces.

'Okay, then,' Dulcie said, not rising to the bait.

Maisie admired her sister's self-control; their mother was the guilt-trip queen. Thankfully, nothing more was mentioned about Adam, or Maisie's possible return to Birmingham and the family home, and the ad hoc meeting went ahead without further ado.

And with the date now set for the fayre and lots of ideas, Maisie couldn't wait to get stuck in. This spring was shaping up to be the best one ever.

Adam's spirits sank as he spotted two strange cars parked on his parents' drive. He had stupidly assumed that dinner would be a family affair – just him, his mum and his dad – but it looked as though there were going to be at least two additional guests.

Then he recognised one of the cars and his spirits dropped another couple of fathoms.

The Bentley belonged to Linda and Karl Spencer, long-standing friends of his parents. They were nice enough people, he supposed, but not his cup of tea. Linda and his mum enjoyed nothing more than gossiping about various friends and acquaintances or their latest holidays, while Karl and Dad either played the one-upmanship game or talked shop. Dad usually tried to draw Adam into the conversation, but Adam didn't have anything to be one-up about (and if he had, he certainly wouldn't boast about it) and neither was he interested in his dad's accountancy firm.

It looked like he was in for a boring evening, because he suspected the owners of the other car would be equally as— Damn! He had a horrid suspicion he knew who it might be. His mother was a stickler for symmetry and there was no way she would have invited two other couples plus him, because that would mean seven at the table. He would be the odd-man-out, and in his mother's eyes, that would never do.

Which meant that the driver of the Lotus was probably Linda and Karl's daughter, Verity.

Like him, Verity was single. Like him, Verity's parents would be delighted if he and Verity were an item. Although he suspected Verity's parents would only be happy with that unlikely situation if Adam were to join his dad's firm.

Despite Adam being the sole beneficiary when his parents (god forbid) passed on, and would therefore be a wealthy guy, Linda and Karl didn't approve of what he did for a living. A blue-collar worker wasn't what they had in mind as a suitable husband for their only daughter.

Adam had hoped that they would have knocked the idea of him and Verity getting together on the head by now, but if his suspicion was correct and this was indeed Verity's car, then they clearly hadn't given up yet.

In a petty act of defiance, Adam took a second to gather his hair into a man-bun on the top of his head. In his father's eyes, long hair could be kind of forgiven if one pretended that the owner of the hair hadn't had time to visit the barber for a while, but a topknot was a deliberate style (or lack of it) statement.

Adam also unbuttoned the cuffs of this shirt and rolled up the sleeves, displaying several tattoos, and undid the neck of his shirt another notch. Then he moved the van so it was parked immediately next to the gleaming Bently. It was childish of him, but with the prospect of an awkward and boring evening ahead, he had to take his fun where he could find it.

Adam didn't bother ringing the bell, sauntering in to find everyone in the sitting room.

Dad and Karl were standing by the mantlepiece, pre-dinner drinks in hand, and Mum was perched elegantly on the edge of one of the armchairs, her legs neatly crossed at the ankle. Linda and Verity were sitting at either end of one of the sofas.

All of them stopped talking and turned to look when he walked into the room.

'Adam, darling.' His mum rose to her feet in a fluid practised move and greeted him with a kiss on the cheek. Only he could hear her as she hissed, 'You could have made more of an effort.'

'Linda, Karl.' He nodded at his parents' friends. 'This is a surprise. I wasn't expecting anyone else to be here.'

He shook Kevin's hand and pecked Linda on the cheek. Then he turned to Verity and gave her an even briefer peck than he had given her mother.

'I see they've roped you in too,' he said. His smile was sympathetic. Verity was an attractive woman. A year younger than him, she was pretty, self-assured, and polished to an inch of her life from the top of her shiny, expensively cut hair, to the manicured toenails that peeped out from gold high-heeled sandals.

'Drink?' his mum asked. He could tell she was gritting her teeth.

'No, thanks. I'm driving. I'll have a glass of water with the meal.'

'You could always stay the night,' she suggested. 'Then you can let your hair down.' Her wince when she realised that she had drawn attention to his bun, was quickly concealed.

'My, that's an interesting hairstyle, isn't it, Karl?' Linda's face was full of disapproval.

'I think it looks good,' Verity said. 'It suits you. You've got a rock star vibe going on.'

Linda's gaze shot to his hands and the oil that he could never seem to fully wash off, no matter what product he used or how many times he scrubbed them. He sincerely doubted a rockstar would have such workaday hands as his.

Dinner was as cringe-worthy as Adam suspected it would be. The main topic of conversation centred around the proposed merger between his father's and Karl's companies. Karl, it appeared, wanted to take more of a back seat and would be content for Martin to run it. Even Adam, who had zero interest in his dad's company, could see how lucrative it would be for both parties.

He quietly tipped a glass to his father. Good luck to him, he thought, if that was what he wanted. As long as Dad didn't try to rope him in, Adam was happy for him.

As usual when she was hosting a dinner party, his mum had brought in outside caterers and serving staff, so when the meal was over and brandy and coffee were being poured, Adam took the opportunity to slip into the hall and send a quick message to Maisie.

How is your evening?

She was at work, so he didn't expect an answer straight away and was surprised when she sent an immediate response. *Busy. Yours?*

Boring. Dad talking shop. Looking forward to tomorrow evening.

Me too. But I might bore you by talking goat.

You'll never bore me. Adam hesitated, wondering whether he should send it. Would she think it a bit OTT? Then again, he had to say something... He decided to send it, and had just heard the ping of an outgoing message when his mother stepped into the hall.

'There you are! We wondered where you were.' She saw the phone in his hand and her mouth tightened. 'Do you have to play with that constantly?'

'This is the first time this evening.'

'I'm sure your friends could have done without hearing from you until tomorrow.'

'I wasn't on the phone to my friends.'

Her eyes narrowed. 'Please don't tell me it was to do with your so-called job.'

Adam kept his temper with difficulty. 'It's not a **so-called** job. It's a real job. One that pays my bills.'

'One that impinges on your private life,' she snapped.

He almost retorted that at least **he** hadn't been discussing business all evening, but he held his tongue. 'It was nothing to do with work.'

'What was it, then? Are we so boring that you simply had to check your social media page?' She paused and her cross expression lifted. 'Or were you searching for somewhere to take Verity? There's this lovely little restaurant in—'

'I was on the phone to my girlfriend,' he interrupted, aware he was putting the cat amongst the pigeons by mentioning a girlfriend right now, but since Mum clearly wasn't getting the message that he wasn't interested in Verity...

'You have a girlfriend? You never said. Who is she? Do I know her?'

'No, you don't.'

'What's her—?'

The click-clack of high heels stopped his mum in her tracks as Linda approached.

Her gaze raked Adam, then zeroed in on his mum. 'Is everything alright, Sue?' she asked. 'You were gone such a long time that Martin sent me to find you.'

'Everything's fine,' his mum said, taking Linda by the elbow and guiding her back to the dining room.

Adam trailed grudgingly behind, his reluctance increasing when his mother shot him a look, warning him that the conversation was far from over. He wasn't looking forward to being grilled by her, but at least she could start to get used to the idea of him having a girlfriend.

And she might even back off and stop shoving Verity in his face!

CHAPTER SEVEN

'How are the plans for the Easter Fayre coming along?' Adam asked.

Maisie beamed at him and snuggled closer. This was date number eight (or was it nine? – she was starting to lose count) and they were spending it on the hillside overlooking the farm.

Adam had suggested going for a nice long walk, and they were currently sitting side-by-side on a rock, gazing out over the valley below and contemplating whether to have a fish and chip supper later. For some reason (nothing to do with fish and chips as far as Maisie could tell) the subject had swung around to goats, which must have prompted Adam to ask about the forthcoming Easter event.

'Walter and Amos – you remember Amos from the stables?' Maisie asked, and Adam nodded. 'They've been making bunny runs and hutches, and a pen for the chicks. And Petra is lending us Gerald the donkey, and two Shetland ponies for the weekend. Nikki and Sammy have designed posters and I'll be putting them up around the village tomorrow. And—' She paused for breath. 'Dulcie will be wearing a Peter Rabbit costume.'

'That I've got to see.'

'I hope you will. I'll be disappointed if you don't come.'

'Of course I'll come, and I'm happy to help, if you need me.'

'That would be wonderful,' she said cheerfully. 'We've got face-painting planned, an Easter egg hunt, egg decorating, and Otto and Amos will be manning the BBQ. Dulcie is even planning to offer goat milk ice cream. It should be a fun day – fingers crossed.'

'You're enjoying this, aren't you?'

'I am.' Maisie's mood deflated a little as she thought how quickly Easter would arrive. It would soon be here, then the fayre would be over and her help would no longer be needed on the farm.

'What's wrong?' Adam asked. He was so attuned to her moods that she found it hard to hide her feelings from him. Although, so far, she had managed to conceal the fact that she was falling for him more each day. It would be one hell of a wrench to leave him, the farm and

Picklewick behind. So much so, that she was seriously contemplating staying permanently.

Not on the farm obviously, because as Mum had pointed out, it wasn't fair on Dulcie and Otto. Otto, bless him, worked so hard that Dulcie hardly ever saw him; but he was hoping that would change when he hired a second chef. So Maisie wanted to get out of their hair when that happened.

Her problem was, where would she live if not at the farm, and how would she support herself? Her shifts at The Wild Side weren't enough to pay rent on a place of her own.

'I'm thinking about what happens after the Easter Fayre,' she said. 'I expect I'll have to go back to Birmingham, but I don't want to.'

'Why can't you stay here?' He took her hands in his as he turned to face her.

'It was only ever meant to be a temporary visit,' she explained. 'I just needed to get away for a while, to clear my head and work out what I want to do with the rest of my life.'

'And have you?'

'Unfortunately, yes. I say **unfortunately** because I love working on the farm and I don't think there are many of those kinds of jobs in Birmingham city centre.'

'True.'

'Besides, I'm working for bed and board here, and I doubt if I would be able to find the same arrangement anywhere else.'

Adam squeezed her hands. 'What would you do if you went home?'

'Be miserable,' she shot back.

'Then it's a no-brainer. You have to stay here. You have to do what makes you happy.' Adam sounded as though he was speaking from experience. But before she could delve any further, he said, 'How can we make that happen?' and her heart melted that he had said **we,** not **you.**

'Find me a job and a place to live that I can afford?' she joked. 'Oh, and break the news to my mother for me. She won't be happy with me staying in Picklewick. In fact, she'll have a fit.'

'Why?'

'She's been guilting me to go back ever since I got here. She reckons she misses me and she's lonely, but I don't believe it for a minute; she hardly ever saw me when I **was** there. She's been rattling around that house for years. I don't know why she doesn't rent somewhere smaller. When I'm gone for good, it'll be too big for her to live in on her own.'

Maisie shuddered. The thought of having to go back to the city and not see Adam again made her chest ache. She would talk it over with Dulcie, she decided. If she explained how conflicted she was and how desperately she wanted to stay in Picklewick and on the farm, maybe her sister would take pity on her...

Adam had stopped listening. He was squinting into the distance, the beautiful patchwork of fields and copses of trees in the valley below ignored as he thought about what Maisie had just said. He was finding it harder and harder to imagine his life without her in it. She had crept under his skin and burrowed into his heart; he would do anything not to lose her — she **had** to stay.

Slowly an idea began to form. He had a spare room: maybe she could move in with him?

It was a thought... but maybe not a practical or sensible one.

He wasn't sure how she would feel about the suggestion. Heck, he wasn't sure how he felt about it himself. Would she move in as his girlfriend, sharing the same room? Or would he suggest she move into the box room? Both scenarios were fraught with pitfalls. The first meant that they would be living together as a couple and considering they'd not known each other long, moving in **together** seemed rather premature. On the other hand, offering his spare room may suggest a distance he didn't feel.

Either way, he wouldn't expect her to pay anything, so it would give her a chance to get on her feet.

His gaze flickered towards her, then darted away again as something else occurred to him. What if they fell out? Split up? Hated the sight of each other after a couple of months?

He decided not to say anything for now. Maybe Maisie would be able to sort something out for herself. There would be time enough to share his idea with her if – when – she told him she had to return to Birmingham.

'Shall we grab a chippie supper and go to mine?' he said, to break the silence, and she agreed readily.

She had spent a couple of evenings in Adam's flat since that first night when they had come close to making love, although she had yet to stay the night, and having her there felt natural. How she felt about being at his place, he had yet to discover. She seemed at ease though, so maybe moving in (however they decided to play it) wouldn't come as too much of a shock.

It would be strange to have someone else in the flat on a permanent basis, Adam thought, as they drove the short distance to the village to pick up their fish and chips on the way. Although he had lived in shared accommodation when he was in uni, he'd had his little flat all to himself ever since he'd bought the place.

Would he feel awkward having Maisie there? Would it sour their relationship?

Even if it did, he felt compelled to try. If she was in danger of outstaying her welcome at the farm, he would lose her anyway because she would return to Birmingham and that would be the end of it. But if she stayed, their relationship would have a fighting chance.

Out of the blue, another idea occurred to him: **he** didn't have to remain in the flat. He could always move back in with his parents and give Maisie her own space. He would hate living with Mum and Dad, but it would be worth it if it meant that Maisie would stay in Picklewick.

However, it would also mean putting his plans of potentially purchasing Dulcie's derelict farmhouse on hold, but something else would come up sooner or later. He didn't have to put all his eggs in that particular basket.

Adam decided not to mention any of this to either Maisie or his parents just yet. He would wait to see if Maisie was able to persuade Dulcie to let her stay first. That would be his preferred option, because it meant they could carry on as they were and not force their relationship into a direction it wasn't ready to go in just yet.

But despite not wanting to rush things, he was acutely aware that Maisie had crept into his heart and had taken up residence there. For the first time in his life, Adam Haines suspected he might be in love.

The next few days sped past. Maisie was so busy, she didn't have a minute to herself, although she did manage to fit in a few more dates with Adam, and she felt that they were growing closer. So close, that it wouldn't be long before they made love.

Gosh, she was blushing just thinking about it. She had almost given in to her desire on a couple of occasions, but she'd held back, scared of making the commitment, realising that once she gave herself to him completely, her heart would be well and truly lost.

She hadn't spoken to Dulcie yet about the possibility of staying on the farm indefinitely, so that was also preying on her mind. The timing hadn't seemed right, so whilst she waited, she made herself as useful as she possibly could. And so far, it appeared to be working. Dulcie hadn't said anything, but Maisie could see that her sister was relieved to have the routine jobs around the farm done without having to ask, freeing her up to do things such as soap making and organising the Easter Fayre.

Making soap was what Dulcie and Maisie were doing when the farm's landline phone rang in the hall that afternoon, and Dulcie made a face. She was in the kitchen mixing cubes of frozen goats milk with a lye solution, and the disturbance wasn't welcome.

'Can you see who that is?' she asked Maisie, and Maisie hastily removed the rubber gloves and safety goggles she was wearing (lye was horrid stuff!) and went to answer it.

'Dulcie?' Beth shouted.

'Hi, Mum, it's Maisie.'

'Is Dulcie there?'

'She is, but she's up to her elbows making soap. Can I help?'

'No, I just wanted to ask— On second thoughts, it doesn't matter.' And with that, her mum ended the call.

'Who was that?' Dulcie asked when she returned to the kitchen.

'Mum. She said she wanted to ask you something then she hung up.'

'Strange. I dare say she'll call back if it's important. She's probably got a bee in her bonnet about the woman next door again.'

'I try to ignore it,' Maisie said. 'They've been feuding ever since her neighbours moved in.'

'Talking about moving, I'm surprised Mum hasn't thought about renting somewhere smaller,' Dulcie said, echoing what Maisie had said to Adam a few days ago.

Now's my chance, she thought, but as she was considering the best way to phrase things, a small red car chugged into the yard.

'Who is that?' asked Dulcie, peering out of the window through her safety goggles. 'Thank goodness I've almost finished. I've just got to pour it into the mould and— Good grief, is that **Mum?**'

Maisie couldn't believe her eyes either. Their mother was clambering out of the driver's side of the car in a rather ungainly fashion. Her face was almost as red as its paintwork, and her lips were pressed into a thin line.

'What is **she** doing here?' Dulcie demanded. 'I thought you'd just spoken to her?'

'I did.'

'Did you know she was coming?'

Maisie shook her head vehemently. 'Absolutely not.'

They watched Beth stomp across the yard, then turned to each other with wide, disbelieving eyes as the door to the utility room opened.

'Dulcie? Dulcie! I need a hand with—' Beth stopped when she caught sight of her middle daughter. 'What the hell are you wearing?'

'Safety goggles.'

'Why?'

'Because I'm making soap. Mum, what are you doing here?'

'That's a fine welcome, I must say. I've come all this way to see you, and all you can ask is what am I doing here?' She huffed loudly, pulled out one of the kitchen chairs and plopped down onto it.

Maisie winced. Dulcie looked far from happy as she took a deep breath. Maisie could almost see her counting to ten.

'What I meant was,' her sister said after a pause, 'We weren't expecting you. Why didn't you tell me you were coming?'

Their mum's eyes briefly flickered to Maisie, and Maisie guessed she was thinking that if turning up unannounced was good enough for Maisie, then it was good enough for her. Maisie also guessed that if Mum had asked Dulcie whether she could pay her a visit, Dulcie would have tried to talk her out of it.

Maisie felt quite sorry for her sister.

Beth's expression grew sly. 'I thought I would surprise you.'

'You've done that alright,' Dulcie muttered, then she said in a louder voice, 'Why did you phone just now?'

'I couldn't remember where the turn-off to Muddypuddle Lane was, but then I saw it.' She licked her lips. 'Aren't you going to offer your old mum a cup of tea? Oh, and fetch my case from the car, will you?'

Dulcie held up her gloved hands. 'I'm in the middle of something. If you want tea, you'll have to make it yourself.'

'Charming.'

'Mum, this isn't a hotel. If you'd told me you were coming...' She shook her head, her exasperation obvious.

'I'll put the kettle on,' Maisie offered, hoping to diffuse the situation. 'And while it's coming to the boil, I'll fetch your case, Mum.'

Hurrying out to the car, Maisie wondered who it belonged to. Mum had learnt to drive a long time ago, but she didn't own a car. She must have rented it for the journey.

When Maisie caught sight of the size of the case, her eyes bulged. This wasn't an overnight bag; this was an on-holiday-for-a-fortnight jobbie. It was blimmin' heavy, too.

Huffing and puffing, she heaved the case out of the boot and trundled it across the yard and into the house.

'Bloody hell, Mum!' Dulcie exclaimed when she saw it. 'Is the kitchen sink in there? I thought you said you were only staying for a few days.'

Beth sniffed and gazed up at the ceiling. 'A few days, a week – whatever.' She brought her attention back to Dulcie. 'I thought you could do with some help with this Easter thing.'

Dulcie turned back to her soap mixture. 'It's all under control,' she said.

'Another pair of hands is always useful,' Beth insisted. 'Anyway, it'll be nice for us to spend Easter together. It's just a pity Jay can't be with us.'

'The way it's going, I wouldn't be surprised if he turns up out of the blue as well,' Dulcie grumbled.

'Aw, wouldn't that be nice!' Beth crowed.

Maisie was only half listening: she was too busy worrying about how their mum's unexpected arrival would impact on her own hopes to remain on the farm. And she wished she had found an opportunity to speak to Dulcie about it before Mum had turned up, because she definitely couldn't now.

'Anyway,' their mother was saying, 'I'll be here if you need me, and as soon as Easter is out of the way, Maisie and I can travel home together in my brand-new car. Won't that be nice, Maisie?'

Maisie's heart dropped to her feet. That was the last thing she wanted.

Adam was a few minutes early to pick up Maisie this evening. It was either that or be unacceptably late. The job he had been working on had overrun, and he hadn't had time to go home for a shower and a change of clothes, so he'd decided to pick Maisie up on time, then go to his. Considering they were spending the evening snuggling on the sofa with a takeaway and a film, it made sense.

Maisie must have heard him arrive, because her bedroom window opened and she stuck her head out. When she held her hand up, he nodded to show he understood that she would be there in five minutes.

Adam got out and stretched, feeling incredibly stiff. He had been contorting himself into odd shapes to be able to get at an exhaust, and he was extremely grubby to boot. A shower was long overdue.

When the back door opened a minute or so later, he expected to see Maisie, but instead it was Dulcie who walked across the yard towards him. She was followed a second later by an older woman with the same high cheekbones and green-blue eyes, and he guessed she might be Maisie and Dulcie's mother.

'Hiya,' Dulcie said. 'I wondered whether you've had a chance to think about the old farmhouse?'

Adam wasn't sure how to reply. He wanted to put in an offer but he was waiting to see what Maisie intended to do. 'Um, I'm not sure I'm in a position to—' he began, but the woman who had followed Dulcie out of the house interrupted him, saying, 'Aren't you the chap who did the work on the milking whatnot?'

Dulcie's eyes widened and she whirled around. 'Mum, I thought you were supposed to be keeping an eye on the potatoes.'

'They're fine,' the woman said. 'Your name is Adam, isn't it?' She was looking at him with disdain, her nose wrinkled.

He didn't blame her for being less than impressed. He wasn't exactly looking his best right now. Abruptly he wished he had taken the time to go home first. Maisie wouldn't have minded.

Ah, there she was. His heart lifted when he saw her. As usual, she looked gorgeous: her face was glowing and she wore a beaming smile.

It faded when she caught sight of her mother's sour expression. 'I see you've met Adam,' she said.

He held out his hand, glanced at it, saw how dirty and oily it was, had second thoughts and let it drop. 'Nice to meet you, Mrs Fairfax.'

Maisie's mum pressed her lips together.

'Call her Beth,' Maisie said, earning herself a scowl from her mother. Adam thought he had better stick with Mrs

Fairfax for the time being. He nodded to her and smiled.

Her gaze swept over him from the top of his bun to the toes of his worn, muddy work boots and her scowl deepened.

Adam was dismayed: he clearly hadn't made the best of impressions, but hopefully he would be able to rectify that when she got to know him better. **If** she had the opportunity to get to know him better.

He hoped with all his heart that she would, because that meant Maisie would be staying in Picklewick. And the way Adam felt about her, he wanted Maisie to stay more than he had wanted anything else in his life.

Maisie was furious and embarrassed. Her mother's rudeness and obvious dislike of Adam were inexcusable, especially since she had only just met him and knew absolutely nothing about him.

'I'm sorry,' she said stiffly as he drove out of the farmyard. 'My mother can be a bit judgemental at times.'

'It's fine. I'm not exactly looking my best. I should be the one apologising – I came straight from a job to pick you up. If I'd known I was going to meet her, I'd have gone home to shower first.'

Maisie knew it wasn't just Adam's lack of a shower that was responsible for her mum's reaction. And she also heard the faint recrimination in Adam's tone.

'I wish I had known you were going to meet her,' she said. 'She just turned up out of the blue this afternoon. Dulcie wasn't happy.' Neither was Maisie, but she didn't want to go into that right now. 'She's staying until after the Easter Fayre; she says she's here to help, but I reckon she thinks she's missing out, what with Dulcie, Nikki and now me in Picklewick. And since she retired, I think she's bored and lonely.'

'She doesn't look old enough to be retired. What did she do?'

'She used to be a supervisor in a supermarket down the road from where we live. It was handy, because she could walk to work, and when I was younger I used to pop in on my way home from school to beg a couple of pounds for a bag of chips and a can of pop if she was on a late shift.'

'She must miss you.'

'Yeah, she does.' Maisie pulled a face. 'The thing is, I can't live at home forever just to keep her company. I've got my own life to lead.' And she was growing more convinced that she wanted to spend it here in Picklewick.

Her mum turning up and expecting Maisie to travel back with her in less than two weeks, was making her anxious, and she had a feeling that after the Easter Fayre, Dulcie would be glad to see the back of both of them. Maisie didn't blame her: she wouldn't want anyone invading her space if she was all loved-up. And it wasn't as though Dulcie and Otto were an old married couple: they'd got together less than a year ago and their relationship hadn't been plain sailing either. So that meant that if Maisie intended to remain in Picklewick, she needed to find herself another job and somewhere to live a bit sharpish.

A thought occurred to her – did she want to stay here because it was a fresh new start, or did she want to stay because of Adam?

Pushing it to the back of her mind to think about later, she suggested they go to the flat so Adam could get cleaned up, and order a takeaway to be delivered rather than pick one up on the way and risk it going cold whilst he showered.

Maisie wasn't overly hungry, her mother having killed her appetite somewhat, but she guessed Adam would be starving, so as soon as they stepped inside the flat she asked, 'What do you fancy?'

'You.' His eyes widened. 'Sorry, that just slipped out. I don't mind... Whatever you fancy. I'll, er, just go jump in the shower.'

He hurried upstairs, leaving her standing in the living room with a thudding heart and a dry mouth. Maisie heard footsteps above her head, then the sound of the shower running.

Imagining Adam underneath the jet of hot water as it cascaded over his body made her feel faint, and she knew what she wanted to do...

Tingling with a mixture of excitement, fear and desire, Maisie slowly went upstairs, her pulse throbbing at her throat. She was trembling, her palms were damp, and she almost decided to forget the whole thing. And she might well have done, if Adam hadn't stepped out of the bathroom just as she reached the top of the stairs.

He was naked, water droplets glistening on his skin, his modesty only preserved by the towel he was holding to his face which draped over his chest and stomach to his thighs.

Gosh, he's got nice legs, she thought, as her eyes slid down his body.

He froze.

So did she.

His gaze locked onto hers and she couldn't tear herself away. Slowly, deliberately, her fingers crept to the neck of her blouse and she undid the first button. He stared at the exposed flesh and she saw him swallow as she undid another.

When she loosened a third button and the fabric fell open to reveal the lace of her bra, his eyes caught hers again and she inhaled sharply when she saw the raw desire burning in them, a conflagration that threatened to sear her from the inside out.

And when he dropped the towel and opened his arms, she stepped into them with a flame that more than matched his.

CHAPTER EIGHT

'What time do you call this?'

When her mother shouted from the kitchen as Maisie slipped in through the back door of the farmhouse, Maisie had to suppress a shriek of alarm. Her heart thudding, she put a hand to her chest. 'You nearly gave me a heart attack.'

'I've been worried sick.' Beth was sitting at the kitchen table, bundled up in a thick dressing gown, and with socks and fluffy slippers on her feet. Her hands were wrapped around a mug, and she had an aggrieved expression on her face.

'I didn't expect anyone to be up this early,' Maisie said, her heart rate returning to normal as she switched the kettle on. She was gasping for a coffee. After the glorious night she'd had, she needed all the caffeine she could lay her hands on if she didn't want to risk falling asleep in the chicken coop.

'I can see that.' Her mother was positively glowering. 'You stayed out all night.'

'Yes, I did.' Maisie was unable to suppress a smile. She was glowing inside, and she was so happy she could burst. Last night had been wonderful. **Adam** had been wonderful. Considerate, passionate, loving...

'It's five-thirty in the morning.' Her mother cut into Maisie's blissful thoughts.

'I know.'

'Dirty stop-out. I didn't raise you to—'
Beth stopped abruptly.

'To what, Mum?' Maisie was becoming
irritated. This was none of her mother's
business.

'To throw yourself at the likes of that
man.'

'By **that man**, I take it you're referring to
Adam.'

'Yes. Him. Did you see the state of him?
He was dirty and covered in oil. And that
hair...' Beth shuddered.

'He'd just finished work,' Maisie
explained, keen to defend him against her
mother's unwarranted attack.

'That's as may be, but it doesn't excuse
his hair and that thing in his eyebrow.'

'It's a piercing.'

'I don't care what it is – it looks awful. The only good thing I can say about it, is that at least it's not through his nose.'

'**You** don't have to like it,' Maisie said through gritted teeth. She took a mug out of the cupboard and smacked it down on the countertop.

'You might have broken that,' her mum grumbled.

'But I didn't. And if I had, I would have bought Dulcie another.' Dulcie would have totally understood. When she had lived at home, stuff had got broken on a regular basis. Their mother had a wonderful knack of winding her daughters up.

How could Maisie go back to that now that she'd had a taste of freedom? The thought made her feel like crying and she vowed to try to speak to Dulcie as soon as possible, although with Mum here, Dulcie wouldn't be in the most amenable of moods.

'I wondered what was keeping you here,' Beth said. 'And now I know. I'm disappointed in you, Maisie; you could do so much better than that grease monkey.'

Grease monkey! Maisie's mouth dropped open. 'I'll have you know he's got his own place and his own business.'

'Dulcie says he lives above an old garage, and from what I can gather, he does a few odd jobs.'

Maisie was flabbergasted. She knew her mum could be opinionated and judgemental, but this was taking it to the extreme. 'You're a fine one to talk,' she spat, anger sparking through her. 'You worked in a shop, and you might live in a house but you don't own it, do you?'

As soon as the words left her lips, Maisie felt awful. Their mum had raised four kids on her own and had done a damned good job of it.

She felt even worse when her mum's chin wobbled as she said, 'That's why I want more for you. Your father was a waste of space – God rest his soul. I don't want you to make the same mistakes I did.'

'I won't, Mum.' Maisie pulled out a chair, sat down, and took her mother's hand. 'Adam's not like that.'

'Nikki has done well for herself, despite that idiot she was married to, and so has Dulcie and Jay. I don't want you to throw your life away on some ne'er-do-well.'

'Adam's not a... whatever you said. He's hard-working and kind, and—' Maisie stopped. 'I think I love him.'

'Huh! How long have you known him?'

'That's irrelevant. Look at Jay and Eliza – within two weeks of them meeting, Jay was jetting off to New Zealand to be with her.'

'That's different,' Beth said, but when Maisie pushed her on it, her mother clammed up and refused to say anything more. 'I'm going back to bed,' she declared. 'I'm too old to be waiting up all night for you to come home.'

'I didn't ask you to,' Maisie muttered.

Beth had the parting shot. 'You kids will be the death of me,' she said, closing the kitchen door firmly behind her and leaving

Maisie feeling as though she had been flattened by a ten-tonne truck.

She wasn't sure whether to feel blessed that she had a mother who cared as much as she did, or annoyed that her mum felt it appropriate to interfere in her life, or guilty because she felt she wasn't living up to her mother's aspirations for her.

In the end, annoyance won by a hair when Dulcie came downstairs and told her that far from waiting up all night for Maisie to come home, their mother had slept soundly from ten p.m. until just before Maisie had returned. And the reason Dulcie knew this, was because she had heard Mum snoring when she'd woken to go to the loo. And then Mum had woken **her** up at just gone five to complain that Fred, the cockerel that belonged to the stables, had disturbed her with its crowing.

If Maisie hadn't already vowed to do her utmost not to return to Birmingham and her mum's house, she would definitely have made up her mind after hearing that!

Adam was on cloud ten: cloud nine wasn't high enough. He felt as though he was walking on a fluffy cloud of marsh mallows, and his heart felt just as gooey. Last night had blown his mind, and all he could think about was how soon he could see Maisie again.

However, he was working for the rest of the week, jobs coming in thick and fast (which he certainly wasn't complaining about) and at those times when he was free, Maisie was working in the restaurant.

He was very tempted to wait for her shift to finish this evening and drag her back to the flat to make love to her all night, but both of them needed a good night's sleep after their recent antics, and he was already feeling the effects of lack of sleep: his head was woolly and he kept dropping his tools.

And when his phone rang, making him jump, he dropped that too. Thankfully, it landed on an old rag, so it didn't sustain any damage.

'Hiya, Mum. How are you?'

'I've got a favour to ask. Please hear me out before you say no.'

'How do you know I'm going to say no?'

'Because it involves Verity.'

'Ah.'

'See? That's what I mean.'

He uttered a sigh. 'What's the favour?'

'As you know, your father and Karl have been discussing a merger... Oh, I do wish you'd come on board. It would mean the world to him!'

'Mum, we've been over this.'

'I know, but—' She stopped and he guessed she would have been quite happy to go over the same old ground if it wasn't for this favour she wanted to ask. 'Anyway,' she continued, 'We'll come back to that another time. On Saturday your father and I are having Karl, Linda, his board members and their wives or partners over for dinner, and Karl believes they will be far more amenable to the merger if they can see that your father is supported by his family.'

'What's that got to do with it? It's not as though you or I have any say in how the business is run.'

'You could, if you wanted.'

'Mum...'

'Just come, please. Show your support.'

Adam wanted to say no, as he had been hoping to see Maisie on Saturday because she had the day off, but although his mum and dad were often on his back about the way he lived and his career choice, they rarely asked him for anything, and although he wasn't interested in the business per se, he knew how much it meant to his dad. His father lived and breathed it; it was what made him tick

'I'll be there,' he promised reluctantly. He was disappointed not to be spending Saturday evening with Maisie, but maybe they could spend the day together instead. It would be better than not seeing her at all.

For the first time since she'd arrived at the farm, Maisie was at a loose end. She'd had a lovely morning with Adam, pottering around the shops in Thornbury and having a spot of lunch in a cafe in the town. Then they'd gone back to his flat and— She blushed when she thought about the way they had spent the afternoon.

'I wish I didn't have to go to this thing with my parents this evening,' he said, as he dropped her off at the farm. 'I would much rather be with you.'

'Your family is important. I'm sure you'll have a lovely time.'

'I'm sure I won't. The only upside is that the food will be good. What are you going to do with yourself this evening?'

'Watch telly, I expect. And listen to Mum grizzle that there's nothing on.'

She would also have to listen to her mother going on about Adam, but her mum's dislike of the man she had fallen in love with wasn't something Maisie intended to share with him. There would be a showdown soon when Mum realised that Maisie had no intention of going back to Birmingham, and there would be hell to pay. Although how Maisie was going to remain in Picklewick if her sister wanted her gone from the farm, was a problem Maisie had yet to solve. She had already started looking for rooms to rent, but unsurprisingly there wasn't anything in the village. There were a couple in Thornbury, so one of those might have to do for the time being, and there were also more job opportunities in the town than there were in Picklewick.

None of them were what she wanted to do long term, but in the meantime she could gain more experience of working with animals by volunteering. There was a wildlife sanctuary a few miles outside Thornbury, and a rescue home for dogs.

She didn't kid herself that this was going to be easy, but she was determined to give it her best shot. For the first time in her life, Maisie knew what she wanted to do, and she also knew who she wanted to spend it with. All she hoped was that Adam felt the same way – because if he didn't, she didn't know how she could deal with that.

Forcing the negative thoughts away, she brightened. 'I could always go over Dulcie's to-do list and see if there's anything I can help with,' she said. 'Although I think we've got everything in hand.' She clapped her hands. 'Ooh! I can't wait to see the chicks. Dulcie is picking them up on Wednesday. I've never held a baby chicken before.'

She glanced at the barn. It had already been set up in preparation for the Easter weekend, and currently housed three rather sweet bunnies who were getting used to their new home. The goats would shortly join them this evening because Dulcie didn't like the thought of the goatlings being in the meadow all night.

As soon as Adam left, Maisie would fetch them in and round up the chickens so Mr Fox didn't eat them.

'I need a kiss,' Adam declared, pulling her towards him, and Maisie settled into his embrace with a contented sigh. Being in his arms felt so right. It was where she belonged, and she couldn't think of anywhere else she would rather be.

'Change of plan, we're eating out instead,' Adam's mother announced when he walked into his parents' house later that evening. She was coming down the stairs and looked as elegant and expensive as usual. A cloud of perfume wafted over him as she reached the bottom step. 'There was a problem with my usual caterers, so I've booked us into a lovely little restaurant. It's quite new, but it's had the most brilliant reviews.'

Adam had been wondering why there was only his mum and dad's cars on the drive as he'd pulled up in the van.

Slipping a diamond stud into her ear as his dad emerged from the lounge with a glass in his hand, she said, 'Ah, here's your father. Martin, please don't have any more, you're driving.'

'I thought Adam could be our chauffeur for the evening. You don't mind, do you, Adam?'

'Where are we going?' he asked.

'The Wild Side in Picklewick. You might have heard of it?' His mum moved to the large mirror in the hall and leant towards it, turning her head from side to side.

'You could have said; I would have met you there.'

'Ah, but then I would have had to drive myself,' his dad pointed out.

Adam raised his eyes to the ceiling and prayed for patience. If he had known his mother had booked The Wild Side, he wouldn't have agreed to go, despite Maisie not working this evening. He ought to message her and tell her—

'Adam, put your phone away. We're ready to go.'

Reluctantly Adam slipped his mobile back into his trouser pocket. He was wearing a suit tonight, but no tie. He drew the line at ties, preferring to leave the top button of his shirt undone. He'd spotted his mum's assessing look and her quick frown of displeasure when she'd noticed his tie-less state, but she hadn't said anything. She knew when to pick her battles.

Adam also knew which battles to pick, and arguing over his phone wasn't one of them. He would message Maisie when they got to the restaurant. He might even take a selfie of his bored face and send it to her. Next time he ate there – if there **was** a next time because, let's face it, The Wild Side wasn't cheap and he was trying to save his pennies – he vowed that Maisie would be with him. Although, thinking about it, she mightn't want to eat at the very place she worked, and if that was the case, he could fully understand.

The restaurant was busy when Adam and his parents arrived. At the far end of the room several tables had been pushed together to make one long one, and Adam spied Verity, Linda and Karl, along with three other couples. They all looked at Adam and his parents as they made their way to the table, and Adam noticed with annoyance that the seat next to Verity was vacant.

Verity beamed at him and patted the chair. 'You're next to me,' she said, offering her face to be kissed. She pouted expectantly, but he avoided her lips, pecking at her cheek instead. The pout intensified.

After the introductions were made (Adam biting his tongue when he was referred to as the 'heir apparent' to his dad's firm) he took out his phone once more, only to feel a sharp kick on his ankle.

His mum, who was sitting opposite, glared at him. Adam put it away again.

'So,' one of Karl's directors said to him, 'You'll be taking over your father's company one day? He tells me you're exploring other avenues and gaining business experience beforehand. It's good to have firsthand experience of how businesses operate, don't you think?'

And so it begins, Adam thought, as he tried to formulate a reply that wasn't a deliberate lie, but wouldn't contradict the image of him that his parents wanted to portray. It was going to be a very long evening.

The money would come in handy and Maisie had nothing better to do, so she hastily changed into tailored black trousers and a crisp white blouse, her uniform for The Wild Side.

At least Otto had called **her** first to ask whether she could cover for the member of staff who had phoned in sick, rather than contacting one of the others. He must think she was good at her job, which boosted her confidence that he hadn't given her the job out of pity or a sense of obligation because she was Dulcie's sister.

The other upside, besides the money, was being able to escape from her mum for a few hours, because as soon as Maisie had walked into the farmhouse after Adam had dropped her off, Mum had started moaning, and all because everyone had been too busy to entertain her. Maisie had been out all day, Otto had been finalising his accounts and had set up camp in the smallest of the four bedrooms, Dulcie had been making more soap, and Nikki and Sammy had spent the day with Gio, as they had promised to visit his parents. Therefore, Beth had been on her own for the most part, and hadn't been happy.

The situation was made worse when Walter, her arch-enemy, had turned up with Amos to make some additions to the goats' play area in the meadow. This time, they were installing a seesaw.

The speed with which Dulcie had offered to drive Maisie into the village for her shift at the restaurant, had led Maisie to believe that Dulcie couldn't wait to get out of the house either.

'What does she expect?' Dulcie moaned as her little car bounced down the pitted lane. 'That I would be able to drop everything to keep her amused? Here to help, indeed! She's here because she's bored. Can't you persuade her to do some voluntary work?'

'Since when did she ever listen to me? I'm the daughter who can't hold down a job, remember? She still thinks of me as a kid.'

Dulcie made a noise and Maisie sent her a sharp look.

'I know,' Maisie acknowledged. 'I deserve it. But I'm doing my best to behave like an adult.'

'I must say I'm impressed with how hard you work and what you're willing to do.

Cleaning out the chicken coop isn't pleasant, yet you've done it.'

'Three times,' Maisie said proudly.

'So why can't you keep a job?'

'Because they all involve people.' Maisie's reply came from the heart. She hadn't had to think about it.

Dulcie manoeuvred the car out of Muddypuddle Lane and onto the main road. 'Yet you're doing okay in the restaurant.'

That's because I have to, Maisie thought; being able to stay on the farm depended on it.

Two minutes later the car came to a halt near the restaurant and Maisie got out. 'Thanks for the lift. Enjoy your evening.'

'Wanna swap?'

'No chance!'

'Maybe I'll go for a drive – a long one,' Dulcie grumbled. 'See you later.'

Maisie gave her a wave, then darted up the side street leading to the rear of the restaurant and the staff entrance.

Otto smiled with relief when he saw her. 'It's busy out there. We've got a party of twelve, and every table except for one is booked. Can you do tables one to eight?'

'Sure can,' she said, tying an apron around her waist and stowing her bag in the small back room that also served as an office. She grabbed a pad and pen as Otto told her what was on the specials, finishing with, 'Check with Fleur as to where we are with orders. I don't think table four has ordered yet.'

Table four hadn't, Fleur confirmed when Maisie went into the restaurant area to ask, and she quickly scanned the tables she had been allocated, checking on their drinks status and making sure no one needed her immediate attention.

Satisfied, she was just about to return to the kitchen to see whether any of the starters were ready, when a burst of laughter drew her attention to the large party of diners.

Pleased they were having a good time, her gaze slid away, then snapped back with a jolt.

She could have sworn that was— Yes! **It was! Adam** was a member of the party.

Maisie frowned: she felt certain he'd said he was having a meal at his parents' house, yet here he was, in The Wild Side. He was sitting next to a woman who was half-turned around in her seat and gazing up at him with a love-struck expression on her face. She was also very pretty.

Adam dipped his head towards her and she said something in his ear. It looked incredibly intimate, and when the woman put a hand on his thigh, Maisie gasped in disbelief.

Ignoring the impulse to march over there and demand to know what was going on, she dashed to the ladies' loos. There was probably a perfectly good explanation, but she needed to compose herself before she heard it. She would take a minute, then she would go back out there and casually saunter up to the table and ask whether anyone needed anything. She would try to act normally and wait for Adam to... **What?** Introduce her? Explain? Ignore her?

But as Maisie dithered, wondering what to do for the best, the outer door to the ladies' loos opened, and on hearing voices she scurried into a cubicle, bolted the door and leant her forehead against it. She wasn't ready to face anyone just yet.

Two sets of heels tapped on the tiles, and the doors to the cubicle to either side of her clicked shut.

She would give it a minute before flushing (so she sounded like a proper loo-user and not some saddo lurking in the toilets), then she would leave.

But what if Adam did ignore her? How was she supposed to react to that?

Nah, don't be silly – he wouldn't do that.

But what if—?

'Adam and Verity make a lovely couple, don't they Sue?' a voice to her left said, breaking into her worried thoughts.

Maisie froze. She straightened up slowly, the blood draining from her face. Surely she had heard incorrectly?

'They do,' the woman on her right replied. 'I'm hoping he'll pop the question before too long, but Adam has still got a few wild oats to sow. I don't think he's **quite** ready to settle down yet.' She tutted. 'When he does, I hope Verity can persuade him to do something about his hair and remove that unsightly hoop he's got in his eyebrow.'

'Oh, I don't know, I think it suits him. And it'll be nice to have some young blood in the boardroom, especially one as good-looking as your son. You must be so proud. He is a real credit to you, and Martin must be thrilled to have Adam follow him into the family business. Let me tell you, John very much wants this merger to go ahead. With Karl intending to step down, the atmosphere in the company has been a bit fraught. It will be nice to know it's in safe hands, especially with Adam ready to step into the driving seat when Martin retires. It's given everyone a real confidence boost.'

A toilet flushed and a door opened, quickly followed by a second flush and the sound of taps being run and hands being washed.

Maisie held her breath. An uncomfortable pressure was building in her chest and she was terrified she might be about to sob. Adam and a woman called Verity? About to pop the question?

How could he? He had **made love** to her, for pity's sake! Had she meant nothing to him?

There was the click of a clasp and she assumed the two women were reapplying their makeup and fluffing up their hair. She prayed for them to leave, before she broke down. This couldn't be happening, she wailed silently. She thought he cared for her, that they had something special.

Adam's betrayal stabbed her in the gut and she felt sick. Not only was she just a 'wild oat to be sown', but he clearly had a girlfriend who was soon to be his fiancée. And he had also lied to her about who he was. Mergers? Boardrooms? Family business? What the hell?!

Maisie realised that she knew nothing about the man she had been sleeping with, the man she had given her heart to, the man she loved.

She had to get out of there right now, before she made a fool of herself in public, and she might have managed to escape with her dignity intact if it hadn't been for one final comment.

'It will be nice to keep it in the family, and Verity is such a lovely young woman,' Adam's mother said.

Maisie lost it. With an anguished cry, she snapped the bolt back and yanked the door open, making the women jump. One of them let out a yelp and placed a hand on her chest, the other backed up a pace or two as Maisie burst out of the cubicle.

She caught sight of her wild eyes and red face in the mirror as she ripped off her apron and threw it at the nearest woman.

'She's sodding welcome to him,' Maisie yelled. 'The two-timing, lying ratbag. I refuse to be anyone's wild oats, and you can tell him that from me!'

Whirling on her heel, she stormed out of the ladies' toilets, ignoring the gasps and a cry of 'Well, I never!' which followed her out.

Tears blurring her vision, she dashed into the kitchen, ran to the office and grabbed her coat and bag. On the way out, she brushed past Otto, who was carrying a couple of plates of food.

'Maisie, where—?'

'Gotta go. Sorry.'

'Are you—?'

She didn't hear the rest of the sentence as she rushed out of the restaurant, because she was too busy trying not to break down completely.

So much for Adam being her prince. He had turned out to be the biggest toad of the lot.

CHAPTER NINE

Adam saw Linda give Karl a nudge and point to something, but he didn't take any notice until he heard Linda say, 'I bet Sue is complaining about something. She usually does.'

He glanced around and when he saw that his mum was speaking to Otto, he cringed. **Please don't let her be making a fuss**, he prayed, making a mental note to apologise to Otto later if necessary.

Her expression was hard, and he guessed that something had irritated her, but what could have annoyed her during a brief trip to the loo was beyond him. But neither was he surprised: his mother could be a very demanding and exacting customer.

He saw her thrust a piece of black cloth at Otto and her lips were moving, but it was impossible to make out what she was saying.

The wife of one of Karl's directors was hovering by her side, looking decidedly uncomfortable, and her gaze kept shooting to Adam and away again.

Adam sent her a sympathetic smile, but she refused to meet his eye.

He wished his mother wouldn't make a fuss. No matter where she went, she always had to complain about something. She wasn't usually as blatant though; a quiet word in the ear of one of the serving staff was usually sufficient. Whatever it was this time, must have really irritated her.

But it was only when Otto looked across the room and his gaze alighted on Adam, did Adam feel a twinge of unease that had nothing to do with embarrassment.

Otto didn't look happy. In fact, he seemed annoyed.

Adam's lips twitched in a half smile, and he hoped he looked suitably apologetic as he gave the chef a little wave. All Otto did was frown and briefly shake his head.

'What?' Adam mouthed, but his mother had reclaimed Otto's attention and Adam's spirits sank even further. He would wait to hear his mother's complaint, then he'd nip off to the loo and message Maisie to warn her that

Otto might be in a bad mood when he got home.

When his mum returned to the table, Adam was about to ask her what was going on, but his dad got in first.

'What was all that about? The toilet paper not soft enough? The handwash the wrong fragrance?' he quipped.

His mum said, 'You're not going to believe this, but I've just been harangued by a waitress. I think she must have been having some kind of a breakdown, but whatever it was, she yelled at me and then threw her apron in my face.'

'What did you do to upset her?' Martin asked.

Sue glared at him. 'Nothing. We were powdering our noses and she burst out of one of the cubicles, shouting something about how 'she's welcome to him' and that she isn't anyone's 'wild oats'. I mean, honestly! They should have a separate toilet for staff. She was quite deranged.'

The director's wife added, looking straight at Adam, 'What was odd was that she seemed to know **you**.'

Adam was beginning to get a very bad feeling about this. 'How so?'

'She referred to someone as a two-timing, lying ratbag and said that your mother could tell you that. Or words to that effect.'

The bad feeling was getting worse. 'Mum, what did she look like?'

'I don't know. What does it matter?'

'How old was she? Did she have blonde hair?'

His mother shrugged, but the director's wife said, 'Mid-twenties, maybe? And she did have blonde hair, now that I come to think about it. Do you know her?'

Adam had a sinking feeling that he did, and he retrieved his phone from his pocket.

'Adam, not at the table,' his mother scolded.

His phone to his ear, Adam got to his feet and headed towards the door.

His call went unanswered. As did a second one.

Dread creeping through his veins, he grabbed the attention of a waitress.

'Please tell me Maisie isn't working this evening,' he pleaded.

'She wasn't supposed to be, but someone called in sick so Chef asked her to step in.'

'Can you go get her for me?'

'Sorry, she walked out. She had a run-in with one of your party.' The waitress narrowed her eyes.

'Do you know what it was about?'

A shrug. 'No idea, but she was crying when she left.'

Adam didn't bother to return to the table to ask what the run-in was about; he would find out soon enough when he caught up with Maisie. She was his only concern now, as he hurried outside after her, confident that she couldn't have gone far.

Her heart breaking, Maisie pelted along the high street, ignoring the curious stares from the people she passed. She also ignored the phone call from Adam and she turned her phone off, not wanting to hear his excuses. She didn't want to see him, speak to him, or hear his name mentioned ever again.

Tears poured down her face and her breath came in gasping sobs as she fled towards the outskirts of the village and the path that would take her through the fields and up to the farm.

All she could think about was how badly Adam had deceived her. She had only managed a quick glimpse at his girlfriend, but from what Maisie could remember she was gorgeous. And all over him. They were clearly an item. The woman in the loo had said as much. For god's sake, she had said that she was expecting him to propose soon!

And far from being a man who was struggling to grow his business, Adam was loaded. Or his parents were, which amounted to the same thing. Did he get his kicks out of pretending to be poor when he so obviously wasn't?

Maisie paused to catch her breath; the hill was steep and she could hardly breathe for crying. With shaking fingers, she brushed away the tears, then fished in her bag for a tissue to blow her nose. Resuming her journey more slowly, a pang of guilt went through her as she realised she had left Otto in the lurch. He didn't deserve that, but there was no way she could have carried on serving this evening.

And after this, she guessed she wouldn't be serving at The Wild Side on any other evening either.

But that was okay, she didn't intend to. She was going to leave the farm and Picklewick first thing in the morning. Mum could come with her, or not. Maisie honestly didn't care. Even if she hadn't burned her bridges with Dulcie, she couldn't contemplate remaining in the village. The thought of bumping into Adam made her feel sick. There was nothing for her here now.

Maisie wasn't sure there ever had been.

The dream of living in Picklewick and working with animals, had been just that

– a dream. And now it had turned into a nightmare.

She would go back to Birmingham where she belonged.

A bitter laugh escaped her. Her mother had been right: Adam **wasn't** good enough for her. But she had been right for all the wrong reasons. Adam wasn't a ne'er-do-well. Adam was an entitled, doing-very-well-for-himself two-timing ratbag.

'What the hell did you say to her?' Adam hissed in his mum's ear. He had searched up and down the high street but Maisie was nowhere in sight, so he had returned to the restaurant to find out what had happened.

Maisie wasn't answering his calls and she hadn't read his messages either, and he was frantic with worry.

'Can we not do this now, please?' His mother's tone was frosty, and she gave him a meaningful glare.

'I want to know,' he insisted.

'Why?'

'Because you must have said something to upset her.'

His mother removed her napkin from her lap and got to her feet. 'Excuse us a moment, won't you? Martin, order some more wine. We won't be long.' She grabbed Adam by the elbow and steered him into the foyer. 'I would appreciate it if you didn't speak to me like that,' she began, but Adam cut her off.

'What did you say to Maisie?'

'Nothing. Not one word. **She** spoke to **me**, and very rude she was, too.'

'You must have said **something.**'

'Are you calling me a liar, Adam?'

'Not at all.' He raised his hand to run his fingers through his hair, before realising it was in a bun, so he scratched his head instead. Taking a deep breath, he tried again. 'Tell me what happened.'

'I already did. We were powdering our noses and chatting about the merger, and saying that you and Verity were a lovely couple, when this woman burst out of a cubicle and started shouting.' His mother stopped, and her eyes widened. 'Oh, my god! Was that woman your girlfriend? I thought you were making it up to annoy me.'

Adam felt sick. He could all too easily imagine the conversation, and Maisie's reaction on hearing it. No wonder she was upset. He had to talk to her and explain.

He turned to leave, just as his mother said, '**A waitress?**' Her tone was scornful.

'Yes.' His anger was beginning to build.

'But what about Verity?'

'What about her? I've told you before, I have zero interest in Verity. Even if I didn't love Maisie, I wouldn't date Verity.'

'**Love?** Adam, please, you don't mean it?'

'I do.' Hearing footsteps, he turned to see his dad approaching and groaned. He could do without a lecture from his father.

His mother was spluttering with indignation. 'Did you hear what Adam just said? He thinks he's in love with that waitress – the one that was so abusive.'

'Nonsense,' his father scoffed. 'He can't be. I won't allow it.'

'That's enough!' Adam shouted, losing his temper. 'What do you mean **you won't allow it**? It's not up to you who I fall in love with. It's none of your business.'

'Your mother and I are fed up with you making a hash of your life. You've got a wonderful future ahead of you, with a young lady who thinks the world of you, yet you're willing to throw it all away to muck about with engines and chase a piece of skirt.'

'I'm throwing nothing away,' Adam retorted.

His father scowled and drew himself up to his full height, anger flashing in his eyes.

Adam wasn't impressed.

He was even less impressed when his father issued an ultimatum. 'Either you get rid of this stupid notion of being in love, or I'll disown you. Your choice.'

Dulcie was incandescent with rage. 'How dare you! I warned you, didn't I? I told you that if you got up to your old tricks in Otto's restaurant, you would be out on your ear. If it wasn't too late to catch a train, I'd drive you to the station this very minute.'

Maisie hung her head. The tirade had begun as soon as she'd entered the farmhouse to find Dulcie and Mum waiting in the kitchen. Dulcie's expression was apoplectic. Their mother's was smug. Beth usually looked resigned and disappointed when Maisie lost a job, but Maisie guessed Mum was happy this time because it meant there was no danger of her staying on the farm now.

'What the hell happened?' Dulcie demanded. 'Otto told me you insulted a diner, then walked out.'

With fresh tears in her eyes, Maisie said, 'Did he tell you that Adam was there with his girlfriend, soon to be his fiancée?'

'What? No! But aren't you two—?'

'Yeah, that's what I thought too. Apparently not. He was having dinner with her, his mother and some others. His mother was talking about how she expected him to pop the question any day now.' Maisie put a hand to her mouth to hold back a wail of anguish.

'No, Otto didn't tell me that, but it's beside the point. You shouldn't have insulted her. This is Otto's livelihood, and you're damaging it.'

'I know and I'm sorry, but I couldn't stand there and listen—'

'Yes, you could.' Dulcie was adamant. 'That's what being a grown-up is all about, Maisie. Control.' She shook her head. 'I shouldn't have expected anything different from you. It's not as though you haven't got a track record of walking out of jobs. Or dumping boyfriends, for that matter.'

'I told you he was no good,' Beth chimed in. 'I could tell as soon as I set eyes on him.'

'Yeah, right,' Maisie said bitterly.

'I said he was nothing but a grease monkey.' Beth folded her arms, her satisfaction evident.

Maisie said, 'It's the opposite, in fact, Mum.'

'Eh?'

'It doesn't matter.' Nothing mattered anymore. Maisie just wanted to find a dark corner and curl up in it until she recovered from her misery. If she ever did. 'I'll go and pack. If one of you could give me a lift to Thornbury, I can be out of your hair tonight.'

Dulcie said, 'Don't be silly. You won't get a train at this time of night.'

'Don't care.'

'Grow up!' her sister snapped. 'You can't wait on the platform all night.'

'I'm not planning to. I'll find a hotel.'

A hammering on the door made all three jump. 'Maisie? Maisie! Open up. I need to speak with you.'

'That's Adam,' Dulcie said.

Maisie glowered. 'No shit.'

'Watch your language, Maisie Fairfax,' Beth snapped. 'Leave this to me. I'll give him a piece of my mind.'

'No need. I can give him a piece of my own.' Maisie squared her shoulders. She might be heartbroken and her life, along with her dreams, was falling apart, but she was damned well not going to let Adam see how much she was hurting. 'What do you want?' she demanded, opening the door a crack.

He was out of breath and looked dishevelled. 'To explain.'

'I don't want to hear it. Save your excuses for someone who cares.' She began to close the door and looked down when she met resistance, to find he had his foot in the way. 'If you don't move your foot, I'll break it,' she warned.

'Verity isn't my girlfriend. We are not a couple. We never have been and never will be, despite my mother wishing we were.'

'She was all over you.'

'Was she? I didn't notice.'

'She had her hand on your leg. And the look on her face...'

'What look?'

'Love.'

'I didn't notice that, either. And do you know why? Because I've only got eyes for **you**.'

'Don't listen to him,' Beth shouted from the kitchen.

'I'm not,' Maisie called back. But she didn't close the door.

Adam said, 'Her parents and mine have been friends ever since I can remember. Mum and Linda had this stupid idea that we would get married, despite me telling Mum I don't think of Verity in that way. I thought she'd got the message but since the talk of a merger—'

'Ah yes, let's don't forget **the merger**. You're going to be on the board of directors.'

'No, I'm not. I never wanted to be an accountant and I don't want to join my father's firm. Look, I don't care whether it's a two-bit outfit with an office above the chip shop, or a multi-million-pound company, I'm not interested. I told them that. And I told them again that there'll never be anything between Verity and me. You are my girlfriend and I love **you**, so I don't care about them disowning me.' He stopped and stared at her.

Maisie blinked. Her eyes felt raw and gritty, and she was weary to the bone. But there was a little nugget in that speech that perked her up no end.

'Did you just say you love me?' she demanded.

He hung his head and nodded, then peered at her from underneath those luscious lashes of his.

Maisie's heart began to sing, and she opened the door wider. **He loved her**! He'd just said so!

But she realised he had also said something else: something she couldn't ignore. 'Are your parents really going to disown you if we carry on seeing each other?'

'It's just Dad blowing off steam. He'll come around, and even if he doesn't, it doesn't matter. I don't need them or their money. What I need is **you**.'

'But they are your parents.'

'So? You are my girlfriend. I love you.' He swallowed. 'I know you accused me of being a lying, cheating ratbag—'

'You are!' Beth shouted.

'But I haven't cheated or lied,' he insisted.

Beth yelled, 'You're still a ratbag!'

'Mum! Stop it.'

'Well, he is! He's cost you your job.' Her mum came to stand beside her and tried to elbow her out of the way. Maisie stood her ground.

'Is that true?' Adam asked.

'Yes, it is,' Beth said. 'And she's going home with me tomorrow, as Dulcie is throwing her out.'

Dulcie called, 'Stop exaggerating, Mum. I'm not throwing her out. It's about time she went home.'

Beth said, 'She's outstayed her welcome and so have you. Go on, scoot. I told her you were a wrong 'un, and I was right. She can do better than the likes of you.'

Maisie wanted to tell her mum to bugger off. She wanted to tell Adam that he definitely wasn't a wrong 'un, and that she absolutely couldn't do any better, but she didn't. She recalled how posh his mother's accent was, the way she had spoken, her expensive clothes and the diamonds glinting at her throat and in her ears. Adam's family were clearly wealthy, and because of her, his parents were threatening to disown him.

She couldn't let that happen. He might think he didn't care, but at some point he would. And she had no intention of being the cause of a rift between Adam and his family.

She told him as much, then she closed the door as he tried to convince her he didn't care about his parents. But he *did* care, and she knew she was doing the right thing.

Letting him walk away, shoulders hunched and head bowed after he had declared his love for her and had been rejected, was the hardest thing she had ever done.

As she lay awake all through the night, Maisie vowed never to let anyone else touch her heart the way Adam had. How could she, when it was shattered into hundreds of pieces and strewn across the misery that her life had become.

How do you carry on when the stuffing has been knocked out of you? One day at a time, Adam decided the next morning, after having absolutely no sleep whatsoever.

He hadn't wanted to get out of bed, despite not actually having managed any sleep, but a sense of obligation to his client this morning forced him to move.

Not bothering with breakfast, he had a desultory shower to try to wash away the smell of despair that lingered on his skin, and it was only when he looked for his keys did he remember that he had left the van at his parents' house and had been forced to use the spare key hidden under a pot at the rear of his flat to get in last night.

Damn and blast. He had no choice but to go fetch it. All he hoped was that his dad would have left for the office by the time he got there. In an ideal world, his mum would also be out, but he didn't usually have that kind of luck.

He was debating whether he should phone for a taxi or walk, when movement outside his living room window made him pause. His van had pulled into the area in front of the garage, followed by his father's car. He could see Mum in the driver's seat, which must mean that his father had driven the van.

Oh, well, it saved him a journey, he supposed.

Hoping that his father would simply post the keys through the letter box and be on his way, he was disappointed when there was a knock on the door.

Reluctantly he went downstairs to answer it.

'You look like death warmed up,' his father observed. 'I've brought you the van. I thought you might need it.'

'Thanks.'

'About yesterday evening... I meant what I said.'

Adam stared at him dully. He didn't care whether they disowned him or not: the damage was done. Through his parents' stupid insistence that he would grow out of wanting to mend machines and would come to work in the family business, they had managed to drive away the woman he loved. If his father hadn't issued such a draconian ultimatum, and if Adam hadn't told Maisie, she would still be in Picklewick.

Or would she?

With Dulcie 'throwing her out' and Maisie no longer having a job, she might have insisted on returning to Birmingham anyway. After all, she hadn't said she loved him back, so that meant she probably didn't.

He'd made a right fool of himself, hadn't he?

But that didn't hurt nearly as much as his broken heart. Adam had never known pain like it and he hoped he never would again.

Wordlessly, he held his hand out for the keys to the van, and with a shrug his father dropped them into his open palm.

It looked like his dad was sticking to his guns, but that was okay, because Adam intended to stick to his too. Dad had to learn that he couldn't bully him. All Adam had left now was his business, and there was no way he was giving it up. It was the only light in what was a very long and dark tunnel ahead.

When a sleek black SUV pulled up alongside the van, Adam barely noticed, too wrapped up in his misery.

But he did a double-take when Otto got out of it.

'Mr Haines, Mrs Haines, good morning.' Otto waved at Adam's mum, who was still in the car. 'I hope the meal was to your satisfaction.'

Martin's reply was stiff. 'It was. Eventually.'

'Excellent.'

Adam's mum emerged from the car. 'I hope you're here to apologise to my son.'

'Not at all. I'm here to tell him that Maisie and her mother won't be going anywhere for a while. Car trouble.' Otto had a gleam in his eye. 'They'll need someone to take a look.'

'Phone a garage.' Adam's tone was wooden.

'Beth did. No joy.'

'Breakdown cover?'

'She hasn't got any.'

'Am I being set up?'

'Maybe.'

'What good will it do? Maisie is determined to go home.' Adam noticed that his parents were following the exchange closely.

'She'll regret it. Anyway, her home is here, in Picklewick.'

'Dulcie mightn't agree with you.'

'Dulcie is a romantic at heart.'

'What about Beth?'

'So is she. That's where Dulcie gets it from.'

'You could have fooled me.'

'Ultimately, she wants Maisie to be happy.'

'As do I,' Adam said.

'What about **your** happiness?'

'Mine doesn't matter.'

'I think it does. Don't you agree, Mr Haines?'

'Yes, but—'

'What about you, Mrs Haines? Don't you think Adam's happiness is important?'

His mother didn't reply, but Adam could see the cogs turning.

His dad began to bluster. 'I think I know what's best for my son.'

'Do you, Dad?' Adam's tone was steady, but inside he was seething. His parents clearly didn't give a jot whether he was happy or not, as long as he did what was expected of him. 'I'll come take a look at that car,' he said.

'Is that woman really leaving Picklewick?' his mother demanded.

Otto said, 'She will if Adam doesn't convince her to stay. She told me about you and Mr Haines making Adam choose between the woman he loves and the parents who don't love him enough.'

Martin took a step towards Otto. 'How dare you! I love my son unconditionally.'

Otto raised his eyebrows.

Adam's father subsided, flushing bright red as he realised what he had said.

'Martin, I don't want to lose him,' his mum cried. 'He's my **son**.'

Adam turned to her. 'You don't have to lose me, but you must trust me to know what's best for **me**. You've got to let me live my life the way I want to live it.' He looked at his father. 'I'm sorry Dad, but I hate accounting.'

Martin rolled his eyes. 'Now he tells me.'

'I did try to tell you years ago, but you wouldn't listen.'

'Do you really love this woman?'

'Maisie. Her name is **Maisie**. Yes, I do. With all my heart.'

He waited for his parents to say something – anything – but when they didn't, his heart sank. It looked like they were still intent on disowning him, which made trying to convince Maisie to come back to him almost impossible. She had been willing to end it, rather than cause a rift between him and his parents. That rift wasn't going to go away, it seemed.

But then his father said, 'What are you waiting for, Adam? Haven't you got an engine to fix?'

And Adam felt a wild surge of hope as he jumped in the van and followed Otto up Muddypuddle Lane towards the farm and the woman who had stolen his heart.

Engines clearly weren't either Maisie's or her mum's strong point and despite opening the bonnet and peering hopefully inside, the car had continued to refuse to start. Turning the engine over repeatedly had resulted in a flat battery, and now the damned thing was completely dead.

'I might know someone,' Otto had said. 'His number is down at the cottage. I'll call him on the way to the restaurant.'

'You're going in early,' Beth had observed.

'Got things to sort out.'

Maisie and Beth had gone back inside.

'Put the kettle on,' Beth had instructed. 'We might as well have a cuppa while we're waiting. Got any biscuits?'

Maisie had grimaced. The thought of food turned her stomach. Otto had tried to tempt her with some homemade scones earlier, but she'd refused. Bless him, he had done his best to make her feel better, saying that he fully understood her reaction last night, but Maisie still felt awful. He had been so kind, and she had repaid that kindness by causing ructions in his restaurant.

He had found her sitting at the table nursing a cold cup of tea at ten-to-six this morning, and she had ended up telling him all about the overheard conversation, Adam confessing his love for her and that his parents had threatened to disown him, which was why

Maisie felt she had no option but to leave. She couldn't have that on her conscience.

Otto had been incredibly sympathetic, which had made her feel even worse.

Dulcie had calmed down too, Maisie discovered, when her sister had rolled out of bed an hour or so later. Dulcie had even chatted to her as Maisie had stuffed the last few items into her case, telling her that she didn't have to leave if she didn't want to. Dulcie had said that Maisie could stay on the farm indefinitely, but Maisie had insisted she was better off going back to Birmingham.

There was no way she could remain in Picklewick now.

Maisie was sitting at the kitchen table with her hands around yet another cup of untouched tea and was deep in thought, when she felt a touch on her shoulder. Expecting it to be Dulcie or Mum, Maisie almost leapt out of her skin when she saw Adam standing by her elbow.

'What are you doing here?' she gasped, her heart pounding uncomfortably fast.

'You needed someone to look at your mother's car.'

Maisie glanced around the kitchen and realised they were alone. Where was everyone, and who had let him in? If her mother knew he was here, she would run him off the farm with a flea in his ear.

'The keys are in the ignition,' she said, her eyes downcast. She didn't want him to see the pain in them.

'Can we talk?'

'What's the point? It's not going to change anything.'

'You're wrong, it will,' he insisted. 'Otto spoke to my parents this morning.'

'Oh, god. How much apologising did he have to do?' She lifted her head, appalled to think she had caused Otto such a problem. He should have told her: she would have gone with him. **She** was the one who ought to be apologising, not him.

'None. He told them a few home truths.'

Maisie groaned. Instead of making things better, Otto had made it worse.

'Long story short, they are no longer disowning me.' Adam pulled out a chair and sat down opposite. Prising her hands away from the mug, he grasped her fingers. 'Whilst they don't exactly give us their blessing, they're not going to stand in our way. They know I love you.' He squeezed her hands. 'Could you ever feel the same way about me?'

'I can't do this,' she said, snatching them back. 'It's pointless. I've got no job and nowhere to live, so I have to go back with my mum.'

'No, you don't. You can move in with me. If you can't face sharing my bed, or you think it's too soon, you can have the spare room. Hell, I'll move out if I have to, so you can live there on your own.'

'You'd do that for me?'

'In a heartbeat.'

'I don't know what to say.' Maisie was astounded. Her heart was screaming yes, but her head was telling her to slow down and think about it. 'I still don't have a job,' she said, stalling for time. She needed to think. This would be such a big step. There was no doubt that she loved him, but they'd known each other for such a short amount of time...

'You do have a job. Otto isn't going to sack you. He told me so. And you won't have to pay rent or help with the bills, or...' Adam trailed off. '**Please**. I can't bear to lose you. You've got to stay.'

'I've already told her that she can stay here,' Dulcie said, appearing in the doorway. 'I still need help around the farm. Maisie, nothing needs to change. You don't have to go home with Mum and neither do you have to move in with Adam if you're not ready. This can be your home for as long as you want it to be.'

'But what about you and Otto? You need your alone time.'

Dulcie twinkled at her. 'Don't worry about us, we get plenty of **alone time**. Anyway, I get the feeling you'll be spending more time at Adam's place than you will here. There's just one thing...'

'What?' Maisie knew there would be a catch.

'You need to put this guy out of his misery and tell him you love him. You **do** love him, don't you, Maisie?'

'I do!' She clapped her hands together, joy surging through her.

'Then I think you'd better tell him,' Dulcie advised.

Maisie went one better: she threw herself at him and kissed him so soundly that she hoped he was in no doubt how she felt about him. **Then** she told him.

'We need more sausages and more bread rolls,' Maisie announced, dashing into the kitchen. 'Otto sent me to fetch them.'

Nikki reached into the fridge, which was looking decidedly emptier than it had done this morning when it had been crammed full of sausages, burgers and Otto's secret hot sauce.

'Here,' Nikki said, thrusting several packets of sausages into Maisie's hands. 'I'll bring the rolls.' They were stacked on the dining room table, and there was now only half the amount that they'd started with.

Maisie hurried out into the yard, where Amos and Otto were manning the barbeque. The farm was thronging with people, mainly families, and Maisie was delighted for Dulcie. The baby animals were the highlights, although the Easter egg hunt had proved popular, and the egg painting was still in full swing. The Shetland ponies were giving rides around the field, led by Petra and October, who worked at the stables, and Walter had been roped into driving the tractor which pulled a trailer for a different kind of ride around the farm.

And then there was Dulcie, who was dressed in a Peter Rabbit costume. She was the biggest hit with the younger children, and as far as Maisie could tell, her sister was having the time of her life. Even Mum seemed to be enjoying herself, chatting with the visitors and directing them to the various activities.

Overall, the Easter Fayre was a roaring success, and Maisie felt proud that she had helped make it happen. But even as she rushed around, helping out here, there and everywhere, part of her was thinking ahead to the next event in the farm's calendar, which would be the sunflower maze in the summer. The seeds would have to be sown in the next couple of weeks, which meant that the ground would shortly have to be prepared. Not only that, the proposed pumpkin patch also needed to be worked over before sowing those seeds too.

Adam, surprisingly, was doing a goat-milking demonstration, then giving out samples of the pasteurised result for visitors to taste, and Maisie paused for a moment to watch, her heart bursting with love.

Soon she would take Adam up on his offer to move in with him – but not into his spare room. If she was going to live with a man, she was going to do it **properly**. The thought made her tingle all over.

The rest of the day was filled with frantic activity and didn't end until long after the last of the visitors had left and the clean-up operation was complete.

Tired but happy, Maisie joined her family in the dining room for a bowl of the curry that Otto had made, and a glass of wine to celebrate a job well done. She had just done a final check on the animals and was the last to sit down at the table.

Dulcie called for quiet before everyone tucked in. 'We just want to say thank you for all your help,' she announced, taking hold of Otto's hand and gazing around the room. 'We couldn't have done it without you, and I'm already looking forward to the next one,' she added, and everyone groaned good-naturedly. 'Before you start filling your faces with Otto's delicious curry, I also want to tell you that I've sold the old farmhouse, so we've got a bit of extra cash to play with.'

'Who to?' Nikki asked, her fork poised above her bowl. 'I thought you were going to give it to Jay.'

'He didn't want it. However, Adam **did**. We're signing the contracts next week.'

Maisie was stunned. He'd kept that quiet; so had Dulcie, for that matter.

Adam said, 'It's going to take a lot of time and money to make it habitable, but it'll be fantastic when it's done. I'll have room for my workshop, and Maisie will have room for her kennels, or a cattery, or a wildlife sanctuary – or whatever she wants to do.'

Maisie was stunned. 'Do you mean that?'

'I do, but it's going to be hard work,' he warned.

'I don't care!' Maisie cried, throwing her arms around him. 'This is a dream come true.'

She had never been so happy. With a wonderful man by her side and a bright future ahead, she couldn't wait to get started.

Maisie Fairfax had kissed her last frog!

There are loads more large print books in the Muddypuddle Lane series. Available at all good book stores, or ask your local library.

About Etti

Etti Summers is the author of wonderfully romantic fiction with happy ever afters guaranteed.

She is also a wife, a mum, a pink gin enthusiast, a veggie grower and a keen reader.

Milton Keynes UK
Ingram Content Group UK Ltd.
UKHW040826250224
438359UK00004B/182